Partia
Upd

Partial Connections

UPDATED EDITION

Marilyn Strathern

A Division of
ROWMAN & LITTLEFIELD PUBLISHERS, INC.
Walnut Creek • Lanham • New York • Toronto • Oxford

ALTAMIRA PRESS
A division of Rowman & Littlefield Publishers, Inc.
1630 North Main Street, #367
Walnut Creek, CA 94596
www.altamirapress.com

Rowman & Littlefield Publishers, Inc.
A wholly owned subsidary of The Rowman & Littlefield Publishing Group, Inc.
4501 Forbes Boulevard, Suite 200
Lanham, MD 20706

PO Box 317
Oxford
OX2 9RU, UK

British Library Cataloguing in Publication Information Available
A previous edition of this book was catalogued as follows by the Library of Congress:

Strathern, Marilyn.
    Partial Connections / Marilyn Strathern.
        p. cm.—(ASAO special publications ; no. 3)
    Includes bibliographical references and index
    1. Ethnology—Authorship. 2. Ethnology—Philosophy. 3. Ethnology—
Melanesia. 4. Melanesia—Social life and customs. I. Title. II. Series
GN307.7.S77 1991
305.8001—dc20   90-20631 CIP

ISBN 0-7591-0759-9 (alk. paper)
ISBN 0-7591-0760-2 (pbk. : alk. paper)

Printed in the United States of America

For M.F.D

Such a grand idea deserves to be widely known and so demands exposition at every level.

Michael Berry: review of Ian Stewart's book on the mathematics of chaos, **The Times Higher Educational Supplement** 30-vi-89.[1] The grand idea is the discovery that the laws of physics contain their own unpredictability or intermittency effect.

PARTIAL CONNECTIONS

CONTENTS

WRITING ANTHROPOLOGY

1. AESTHETICS <u>Ethnography as Evocation</u>

    1. EVOCATION

        Representation and evocation
        Aesthetic impasse

    2. JOURNEY

        The anti-aesthetic break
        A hidden form

    <u>Complex Society, Incomplete Knowledge</u>

    1. RETURNED

        Complex pasts
        Cosmopolitans

    2. PLACED

        Sharing villages
        Awkward presences

2. POLITICS <u>Feminist Critique</u>

    1. VOICES

        Interest groups
        Partial participants

    2. BODIES

        One is too few but two are too many
        A hidden extension

    <u>Intrusions and Comparisons</u>

    1. INTRUSIONS

        Techniques of control
        Cross-cultural impasse

    2. COMPARISONS

        Units for comparative analysis
        Partial connections

PARTIAL CONNECTIONS

WRITING ANTHROPOLOGY

This narrative is organized in response to a narrative problem. I wished to take the reader through various 'positions' that have recently marked changing anthropological approaches to writing and representation in ethnography, in order to create a position from which to reconsider the possibility of cross-cultural comparison for Melanesia. But it seemed impossible to divide the work without appearing to give disproportionate weight to one or other dimension. Either the theoretical excursus would seem like an introduction to the comparative issues, or the latter would seem mere appendix to the former. The one could implicate the whole of the discipline where the other concerns only a small region of the world; conversely, the one focuses on a particular instrument of endeavor where the other could offer concrete data in their realistic totality. Yet each might be equally subject to complex argument.

Since this problem of proportion also appears in the anthropologist's confrontation with the complexity of his or her materials, it seems worth exploration. More than narrative is at stake. Examining the culture of argumentative practice takes us into comparative arguments about the way culture is practised.

$$* \quad * \quad * \quad * \quad * \quad *$$

Complexity is intrinsic to both the ethnographic and comparative enterprise. Anthropologists are concerned to demonstrate the social and cultural entailments of phenomena, though they must in the demonstration simplify the complexity enough to make it visible. What appears to be the object of description — demonstrating complex linkages between elements — also makes description less easy.

Some commonplace, persistent, but also interesting problems lie in the organization of anthropological materials. By organization I refer both to how they are collated and systematized by the observer and how collation and systemization already appear accomplished in the way the actors present their lives. I attend to one set of such problems for the anthropologist, so commonplace that usually we are not troubled by them. For it seems that they would dissolve themselves. It is those problems that are produced by scale, and which scale adjustment should, therefore, resolve.

Thus the question of complexity seems from one point of view a simple matter of scale. The more closely you look, the more detailed things are bound to become. Increase in one dimension (focus) increases the other (detail of data). For example, comparative questions that appear interesting at a distance, on closer inspection may well fragment into a host of subsidiary (and probably more interesting) questions. Complexity thus also comes to be perceived as an artefact of questions asked, and by the same token of boundaries drawn: more complex questions produce more complex answers. Across Melanesia as a whole, it might seem intriguing to look, say, for the presence or absence of initiation practices. When one then starts examining

specific sets of practices, it becomes obvious that 'initiation' is no unitary phenomenon, and there appears to be as broad a gap between different initiatory
practices as between the presence or absence of the practices themselves. As
an effect of scale, all this might seem unremarkable. But it does, in fact,
produce some trouble for the anthropological understanding of the phenomena in question.

The perception of **increasable** complication — that there are always
potentially 'more' things to take into account — contributes to a muted
skepticism about the utility of comparison at all. However, anthropologists do
not produce this sense of complexity unaided. Their discipline has developed
in a cultural milieu committed to ideas of pluralism and enumeration and
with an internal faculty for the perpetual multiplication of things to know.

A cultural account of Western[1] pluralism would address the way a sense
both of diversity and of an increase in the complexity of phenomena is
produced by changing the scale of observation (M. Strathern in press). By
changing scale I mean switching from one perspective[2] on a phenomenon
to another, as anthropologists routinely do in the organization of their materials. It is made possible by a modelling of nature that regards the world
as naturally composed of entities — a multiplicity of individuals or classes or
relationships — whose characteristics are in turn regarded as only ever partially described by analytic schema. Thus one might imagine choosing two
or three elements of initiation practices for theoretical consideration, knowing that for no single case had one grasped the natural character of the entire
phenomenon. Other perspectives remain. This is a version of problems long
familiar to species classification.[3]

At least two orders of perspectives can be readily identified in the way
Westerners take up positions on things. One is the observer's facility to move
between discrete and/or overlapping domains or systems, as one might move
from an economic to a political analysis of (say) ceremonial exchange. The
other is the facility to alter the magnitude of phenomena, from dealing (say)
with a single transaction to dealing with many, or with transactions in a single
society to transactions in many. These orders share an obvious dimension
themselves. The relativizing effect of knowing other perspectives exist gives
the observer a constant sense that any one approach is only ever partial, that
phenomena could be infinitely multiplied.

First, then, relations and connections between entities can appear in new
configurations as one transfers from one domain of enquiry to another, as
an anthropologist might turn from the political-economic dimensions of
ceremonial exchange to its performative and ritual aspects or to its similarity with initiation practices. Second, as entities in themselves, sets of information proliferate as much from the possibility of magnifying the detail of
individual parts as from increasing the whole number of entities being
considered. Changing scale itself thus creates a multiplier effect — whether
we enlarge our purview to consider all the small ritual actions that contrib-

ute to the unfolding of an initiation sequence, or enlarge it to consider such practices from dozens of the now well-documented cases for Papua New Guinea. Perhaps it is the third, concomitant ability to perceive more than one scale at the same time, to move from individual actions to the rite, or from a comparison of several rituals to an exemplification of elements they have in common, or from individual institutions to a configuration, that indeed makes the relations between phenomena appear 'complex'. Complexity is culturally indicated in the ordering or composition of elements that can also be apprehended from the perspective of other orders.

Scale switching not only creates a multiplier effect, it also creates information 'loss'. Different types of data may appear to substitute for one another — a generalization about socialization, say, in lieu of a description of a puberty rite. Information loss appears as the eclipse of detail or of scope by whatever is the present focus of enquiry. It can occur equally through domaining as through magnification or telescoping.

Yet knowing one is switching scales does not prevent a sense of disproportion creeping in. Sometimes this transmits itself as a kind of despair — as when anthropologists alternate between accusing one another now of myopia, now of panoptics. Neither the individual case nor the broad generalization, neither ethnography alone nor analysis alone, neither umbilicus nor globe,[4] seems **sufficient** But sufficient to what? Sufficient perhaps to the intellectual ability to analyze, generalize, expound, in short the activity of description.[5] In the same way, the end product — the monograph, the theory — never seems sufficient to the labor of its production. The capacity for conceptualization, one might say, outruns the concepts it produces.

Let us recast the problem that scale-change itself seems to create, in the switch of perspectives that in creating more also creates less. If, in fact, information is lost proportionate to the new scale of looking at things, and thus proportionate to new information gained, it is apparent that 'the amount' of information has remained the same. Paul Sillitoe's (1988) remarkable compendium of the movable artefacts from Wola in the Southern Highlands of Papua New Guinea runs to as many pages of text as the average whole-society monograph. Or put it this way, similar intellectual operations have to be performed on the data whatever the scale — classification, composition, analysis, discrimination, and so forth. Regardless of the way a change of perspective reveals whole new worlds, the 'same' coordinates of intellectual activity are summoned.

Magnitude provides a simple example. If one thing observed close to appears as perplexing as many things observed from afar, the perplexity itself remains. Each single element that appears to make up the plurality of elements seen from a distance on close inspection turns out to be composed of a similar plurality that demands as comprehensive a treatment. Contrast the Highlands with the Lowlands of Papua New Guinea, and one has to consider the Eastern and Western Highlands, the Southern Highlands and

Mountain Papua, and all the variations between. It is conventional to imagine this scaling as a kind of branching, as though one were dealing with a segmentary lineage system or a genealogical tree, where the more embracing or more remote orders contain derivative or recent ones. But the interesting feature about switching scale is not that one can forever classify into greater or lesser groupings but that at every level complexity replicates itself in scale of detail. 'The same' order of information is repeated, eliciting equivalently complex conceptualization. While we might think that ideas and concepts grow from one another, each idea can also seem a complete universe with its own dimensions, as corrugated and involute as the last.

This may be rephrased as a matter of overlapping dimensions. The amount of information remains, so to speak, despite an increase in the magnitude of detail.

Questions of proportion raised by imagining information as an amount or quantity in turn raise questions about the practice of cross-cultural comparison. We are dealing with a self-perpetuating imagery of complexity; I shall explore aspects of this imagery both in relation to various anthropological arguments and in relation to the perceived diversity of Melanesian cultures and societies. Yet the imagery is not completely self-perpetuating. In the late twentieth century, anthropology has already moved from a plural to what could be called a postplural perception of the world. My account also imitates that move; the realization of the multiplier effect produced by innumerable perspectives extends to the substitutive effect of apprehending that no one perspective offers the totalizing vista it presupposes. It ceases to be perspectival.

*   *   *   *   *   *

As the organization of perspectives on objects of knowledge and enquiry, scale (one might say) behaves the same whatever the scale. Points on a scale can also act as different whole scales. I indicated two orders (domaining, magnification) that yield sets of internal measurements and hence coordinates along which the scale of phenomena may be changed; but as adjuncts to general processes of human perception, these orders behave like so many points along a scale themselves. Thus one may add another order or dimension of perspectives in respect of the different kinds of intellectual activities deployed — as one switches between analysis and explanation, for instance. This particular set of perspectives also affords a perspective from which the other two appear. Domaining and magnification can thus be rendered apparent through the self-consciousness with which images depicting the relationship between different sets of information are deployed in the act of description. Cross-cultural comparison serves as an exemplar of all descriptive activity.

Running through the account has been a recurrent assumption about what comparison entails: the ability, first, to produce generalizations from particular cases; second, to indicate the point at which differences are or are not interesting; and, third, to offer higher order and lower order propositions about the material. Such statements conceived as spatial orderings can be literally applied to geolinguistic grids, as though they corresponded to so many different cartographic areas in the relations between individual cultures and societies. Generalizations can take on the character of an areal configuration into localities and regions. If generalization is thus like a region, a difference is like a social divide, and higher and lower order propositions mobilize images of nearness and distance. As Ann Salmond (1982) pointed out long ago, mapping is a powerful image for the analytical exercise: it has both a domaining and magnifying effect. The colloquialism 'level' combines them both.

Regions and subregions aside, higher and lower order statements can also appear as levels in segmentary classifications or genealogical trees. Taxonomies are often apprehended diagrammatically as a branching or bifurcating of concepts (Thornton 1988a). Here, a kind of genetic relationship is implied in an image of ancestor and offspring. Lower order concepts appear as the outcome of operations performed on higher order ones, as when types are perceived to subdivide. According to the 'generation' at which differences apply, rules of inclusion and exclusion determine the place (the level) of any one element in relation to the principles that generate the whole schema. Such schemas are thus closed by their genetic flow to so speak. To do a componential analysis on the concepts will indicate the application of principles that make each unit part of a domain: a kin term appears as a member of a class of kin terms.

Both images — regional map and bifurcating genealogy — imply certain constancies. The former implies the existence of central points or areas, like so many villages or fields seen from the air, that will remain identifiable however much their features are replotted; all that changes is the perspective of the observer. The latter implies some kind of closure that defines a system of concepts and their potential transformation from within, insofar as only particular trajectories are 'genetically' possible from the principles one starts with. Specifying the features of identity on the one hand and closure on the other provides relative scales for the phenomena so circumscribed.[6] However, certainty in relation to either identity or closure often evaporates in the course of the cross-cultural exercise itself.

Recent examples from Melanesia come to mind. Attempt to produce synthetic configurations from the scrutiny of individual cases runs into the chaotic problem that nothing seems to hold the configuration at the center — there is no map, only endless kaleidoscopic permutations. This is the insight, for instance, with which in the same year both Fredrik Barth (1987) and Daryl Feil (1987) proceeded to elucidate obviously connected yet also differentiated sets of societies in two parts of Papua New Guinea (Mountain Ok and Central Highlands respectively).[7] On the other hand, attempts to produce a typology of societies from the application of constant principles may also

evaporate. For instance, principles of reciprocity as they affect the organization of transactions and the role of leaders as Great Men or Big Men, may
well appear to discriminate effectively between a handful of cases (Godelier
1986); but the discrimination cannot necessarily be sustained at that 'level'
— an expanded version reveals that principles radically distinguishing whole
clusters of societies are also replicated within them (Godelier and Strathern
in press). As a consequence, what distinguishes the Mountain Papuan Baruya
from Hagen in the Central Highlands also appears to the observer to distinguish elder and younger Arapesh brothers in the single settlement of Ilahita
(Tuzin in press).

If a sense of disproportion attends such observations, it can be attributed
to two sources. One is the apparent randomness with which specific values
or features seem to have differential centrality in this or that culture/society.
The other is the disconcerting way in which the same values or features appear
at what otherwise would seem quite incongruent levels in diverse societies/
cultures.

In the first, differential focuses or concerns appear to cut across analytical
domains; in the second, the recurrence of phenomena does not respect the
magnitude of context. In short, phenomena appear to elude scaling. Given
the amount of energy that anthropologists have poured into systematizing
and modelling their data without resolving these issues, neither can be argued
away. On the contrary, they hold considerable interest as cultural phenomena
in themselves. I comment briefly on each in turn.

Much of the control that anthropologists exercise over their data rests
on eliminating alternative perspectives in favor of the one view they adopt.
Thus Barth (1987) and Feil (1987) each in the end concentrate on an exclusive
set of factors. For Barth, it is the religious beliefs of the Mountain Ok people
that are central; for Feil, the productive strategies of wealth accumulation in
the central Highlands. However, the ethnographers' different choices lead to
a sense of disproportion between them. For if 'religion' and 'economics' are
analytical domains, their status and thus their applicability must be independent of the data. The analyst either deploys them or does not. It is barely
logical to suppose that there might be 'more' or 'less' of one or the other
in this or that society. Yet this is often implied in a perceived disparity between
different features of the social and cultural landscape. The analytical domain
is regarded as elucidated by local activities, and some simply appear to present
more detail than others. Thus for the Mountain Ok, religious practice offers
countless variation, and discriminates between the societies of the region in
a way that wealth production does not.

Disproportion arises, then, when the very centers of attention do not hold
steady. What seems central or crucial for one set of societies may appear
incidental or peripheral elsewhere. A result is a disjunction or lack of
connection between what one people regard as a vital focus for their lives,
and what another do. Land tenure here, mythology there: the actors' interests

can appear as out of proportion as the anthropologists'.

However, proportion is not necessarily restored by new perspectives. The idea of perspective suggests one will encounter whole fresh sets of information as one moves through various scales — from organism to cell to atomic particle, from society to group to individual. But a further sense of disproportion is given in those situations where similar sets of data or patternings seemingly recur regardless of scale. Rena Lederman (1986:83) makes the point when she observes that the combination of individual exchange partnerships and corporate clan relations in Mendi society in the Southern Highlands produces a situation in which "it is almost as if counter-poised anthropological models appear together in the actors' reality" (emphasis removed). In other words, models anthropologists have built to discriminate whole societies — as between Hagen and Wiru — may be seemingly replicated in contrasting forms of activity within one of them. Mendi both display valuables in a characteristically 'Hagen' manner, and publicly distribute them with, she says, the clamor of 'Wiru' prestation.

In one sense the replication is an illusion. The manner in which Mendi draw analogies between different levels of their life will be subject to their own perceptions of difference and similarity, to be apprehended in terms of their particular symbolic practices. Mendi motivations quite patently are not those of the anthropologist. But perhaps their techniques are not so dissimilar. Take the common Highlands metonym by which similar features may be attributed to a body of clansmen as are attributed to the body of a single man. If the single man is as complete a description of the clan, as the clan is of a single man, then the 'same' information is recurring at each level. What seems to keep the scale of detail constant is the intellectual activity of the observer/actor. A 'small' thing can thus be made to say as much as a 'big' thing.

To suggest that the 'quantity' of information thereby remains constant is to suggest that the intensity of perception is a constant. The single person is as complex to analyze as a corporation composed of many. But what does not appear disproportionate as a symbolic (e.g. metonymic) device, becomes disproportionate when the replication confounds what are maintained as different levels of information. If the corporation is defined as complex by contrast with the single person, the two cannot be analyzed isomorphically. Or, a higher order discrimination reappears at a lower order which should have been defined in an exclusionary way. In a Great Man as opposed to a Big Man society, one should not be finding differences between Great Men and Big Men!

Yet the surprise is also naive. One might expect certain theoretical interests or explanatory schema to hold good whatever order of data is being examined. Indeed, if one looks beyond anthropology, historians' 'little histories' have been criticized on the grounds that a focus on individual lives and local worlds does not avoid general questions of social change and cultural motivation (Christiansen 1988). If one can ask 'big' questions of 'small' data, then the difference between big and small disappears. It is reinstated only with the reinstatement of perspective and levels, and a concomitant sense of the partial nature of description.

I wish to make the reappearance of similar patterns at different scales evident as an organizational facility of Western pluralist cultural life.[8] But this creates a new realisation of its own. The relativising effect of multiple perspectives will make everything seem partial; the recurrence of similar propositions and bits of information will make everything seem connected. In an experimental vein I artificially reproduce this postplural realization in the organization of the monograph.

Partial connections require images other than those taxonomies or configurations that compel one to look for overarching principles or for core or central features. Clearly, such imagery is not going to take the form of genealogy or map.

*   *   *   *   *   *

Fractal graphics that were for years the arcane province of the science of chaos theory have suddenly acquired a cultural permeability. In Britain, a trade journal such as **The Times Higher Education Supplement** draws on fractal graphics from one book to illustrate reviews of others on different topic (e.g. September 30, 1988; August 25, 1989). The weekend magazine of the national paper, **The Daily Telegraph,** runs a summer number with 'Pictures of Chaos' (August 12, 1989), the feature advertising an exhibition on the popularization of mathematics to be held in Leeds. I walk down the corridor of the Social Anthropology Department in Manchester, and an Africanist greets me with James Gleick's **Chaos** in his hand.

The whorls and involutions of these self-similar shapes that repeat motifs through any scale of magnification produce the most seductive visuals. It is the glistening details of the forms that remain — whether one is looking at the convolutions of clouds or the bifurcations of tree trunks, branches and twigs. These fractal graphics could describe the patterning of maps or genealogies, but they would be maps without centers and genealogies without generations. It is the repetition, the not-quite replication, to which the viewer is compelled to attend.[9]

Probably the best known exemplar is that of the irregular coastline. Whether one looks at a large-scale map or investigates every inlet and rock on a beach, the scale changes make no difference to the amount of irregularity. It is as though increase in the length of coastline does not increase the area it encloses: the two do not map on to each other. Rather, as Gleick puts it, the degree of irregularity as such corresponds to the efficiency of the object in taking up space. This is modelled in the Koch curve known to mathematicians. I quote Gleick:

[a simple, Euclidean] one-dimensional line fills no space at all. But the outline of the Koch curve, with infinite length crowding into finite area, does fill space. It is more than a line, yet less than a plane. It is greater than one-dimensional, yet less than a two-dimensional form (1988:102).

We may think of the amount of irregularity as an amount of detail. To do so recalls the phenomenon observed earlier: despite an increase in the magnitude of detail, the quantity of information an anthropologist derives from what s/he is observing may remain the same. Observation thus remains a kind of constant background to the proliferation of forms.

For present purposes, I dwell on a rather dry image. It looks for all the world like the kind of arid segmentary system by which we imagine regional maps or typological orders, Gleick's rendering of Cantor's dust (1988:93) (see Frontispiece to Section I). However, this neither provides a model for coordinates by which to map cross-cultural data nor indicates generative principles or organization by which to order such data. What it depicts is a repeated irregularity or intermittency, such as telephone engineers find in electrical transmission. Continuous signals are constantly interrupted but at irregular intervals: the scatter of interruptions is not itself continuous. I borrow a single suggestive dimension.

What enables the anthropologist interested in cross-cultural comparison to introduce different levels (scales and points on scales) in his or her schema is the relative containment of comparison or differentiation. Thus, in relative terms, among Papua New Guinean societies the gap between Hagen and Gimi can appear as significant as that between the Highlands and Lowlands, or between Melanesia and Polynesia. The significance depends on the order of detail. Continuities that count at one level — Hagen and Gimi belong to those Highlands societies based on the cultivation of sweet potato and pig-keeping — become irrelevant at another, a necessary progression in the distinction of levels. When horticultural regimes are examined in detail, the few pigs that Gimi capture for their rites seem very different from the large herds that Hageners rear. The contrast is given local emphasis by the fact that Gimi once used pigs as a substitute for hunted marsupials, Hageners in order to dominate the market in imported shell valuables. The order of differentiation is thus held in proportion by the observer at each level.

At the same time, the one simple constant that holds across these scales — whether one is dealing with entire regions or tiny populations, with a complex model of interrelated variables or analysis of a single work process — is that very capacity to differentiate. The intensity of the perception of similarity and difference plays an **equally** significant part in the anthropologists' account whatever the scale. It also appears to play an equally significant part in the actors' orientations.

Differentiation is not after all contained — it runs riot. Significance appears not to depend on order of detail but itself emerges as a constant background to the distinctions at each level. Should we then imagine the activity of comparison or differentiation as having a replicating, self-similar pattern of its own? To say as much would be to attract the scorn generally poured on the idea of ideas generating themselves. So rather than trying to prove the point with data, I shall make data with it.

Take the commonest of relationships, that between the questions anthropologists ask of their material and their answers. We are all too familiar with their never-ending nature. Now insofar as an answer generates new material or insights, then it necessarily draws on knowledge not available to the questioner. For instance, the material needed to consider the presence or absence of initiation rituals exceeds what we know of the rituals themselves; we may be drawn into considering marriage practices as a kind of initiation, or into beliefs about the effectiveness of ritual, or into gender symbolism. This excess may well generate new questions that make the old ones uninteresting. Indeed, we may not even bother to fill in the answers, the new questions seem so much more enticing. Each question in conjunction with its answer, or each position from which a new position is created, in turn becomes a position that one leaves behind. It looks in retrospect (say) as though questions about initiation are a mere subset of what we may then regard as wider or (equally) more precise questions about social reproduction or rationality or patriarchy.

If at each juncture something more is generated than the answer requires, that something more acts as a kind of 'remainder', material that is left over, for it goes beyond the original answer to the question to encapsulate or subdivide that position (the question-and-answer set) by further questions requiring further answers. Or, we might say, it opens up fresh gaps in our understanding.

The image that Gleick produces of the Cantor dust — the apparently increasing sparseness of the particles — is an opening up of gaps. It is not a segmentary model: the levels are not generated by the division of a pre-existing entity into discrete parts through distinction or opposition like a unit dividing or doubling itself, nor does it represent the on/off discrimination of binary digits. Rather, one is made aware of the intermittent nature of intermittency. What is remarkable about the dust is the instruction that creates the burst of points. All that happens is that intervening material is eliminated, a 'gap' or 'background' is revealed.[10] The more frequent the intervals, the more numerous and sparser the points. The result is that, however numerous, the points never exceed the quantity contained in the initial level. And however sparse, they never lose the complexity that the initial level was capable of conveying, for each point is capable of further interruptions. For every piece of information lost, information is gained.

The amount of realisable information does not itself increase or decrease, then; the proliferation or differentiation of detail simply increases one's perception of it. What is involved in proliferation?

Every solid bar produced by the elimination of material, by the emergence of a background, is susceptible itself to the same operation, and indeed never 'exists' as a solid bar. If these were not bursts of errors in an electrical transmission but how a person thought about their thoughts, it might be already knowing this (there is no solid thought) that leads to the proliferation of instructions. Against the solidity of narrative intention, for instance, is the writer's apparent capacity to replicate ideas, jump concepts, and anticipate both possibilities. The Cantor instruction provides an image for the apparently random nature of the bursts of argument by which anthropologists nonetheless organize their accounts. It indicates that there is always a crucial remainder in the possibility that the argument (the instruction) can be repeated on whatever is the result of the previous argument/instruction.

If one considers not just the gaps but how they come to be perceived, we can locate the remaindering effect; the image contains its own remainder, in the act of imagination. As Gleick describes the Cantor dust (his text is on page 2), the self-scaling appearance of the diagram is simply produced by the set of instructions being repeated, each new instruction working from a previous one. Intermittency or discontinuity in the bursts of information is laid out in a sequential form as a pattern of gaps in space and time. The instructions themselves consequently have their own remaindering effect: you are always left with the possibility of repeating them, which means that in addition to every pattern just created (and thereby contained in that pattern) is the further knowledge that patterning could recur. What in effect is repeated at each sequence is the intensity of this perception. 'More' background appears without being enlarged or diminished in amount. The patterns themselves may be regular without being similar, or similar without being regular. It is the possibility of their extension that is entailed in the replication and proliferation.

Replication thought of as repeated instruction is a commonplace in contemporary understandings of the way organisms grow. The effect must be rather like producing gaps in a narrative because of the gaps already there. Let me suppose one could create this effect.

Ideas and arguments are often regarded as 'flowing.' Thus written discourse takes one through a series of positions, even as the different societies or institutions of cross-cultural analysis present a discursive series of re-positionings. The time it might take to travel, as the reader moves through the text, gives a kind of experiential unity to the exercise. Yet this unity or sense of flow or movement is at the same time made up of jumps over gaps, juxtapositions, leaps — unpredictable, irregular. So, continuous as the process of narration might seem, the closer we inspect monographs, paragraphs, sentences, the more aware we are of internal discontinuities. This is the well-known paradox of contacts between surfaces, such as the

> contact between tire treads and concrete [or] . . contact
> in machine joints, or electrical contact. Contacts between
> surfaces have properties quite independent of the mate-
> rials involved. They are properties that turn out to depend
> on the fractal quality of the bumps upon bumps upon
> bumps. One simple but powerful consequence of the fractal
> geometry of surfaces is that surfaces in contact do not touch
> everywhere. The bumpiness at all scales prevents that . . .
> It is why two pieces of a broken teacup can never be re-
> joined, even though they appear to fit together at some
> gross scale. At a smaller scale, irregular bumps are failing
> to coincide.
> (Gleick 1988:106)

Although one's grip on a tool is no less secure because on an infinitesimal scale skin and wood do not touch, the knowledge creates the sensation of there being something else to explain. Certainty itself appears partial, information intermittent. An answer is another question, a connection a gap, a similarity a difference, and vice versa. Wherever we look we are left with the further knowledge that surface understanding conceals gaps and bumps.

Here I try to make explicit the intermittency effect of the intervals or gaps between the sections of the text. They are irregular and unpredictable insofar as they arise from the unfolding (the space-filling) of the arguments themselves. At the same time, proportion should become irrelevant, since the complexity of each burst of argument is held constant. The 'amount' of argument or illustration thus depends on its position, on the space it takes up. Consequently, the exercise is presented as an alternative to the usual kinds of claim to be demonstrating intrinsic connections between disparate parts of one's account. It does, however, draw on real-life debate.

I take as a subject recent arguments on the writing of ethnography within anthropology and the extent to which new formulations assist or resist the task of cross-cultural comparison; they are imagined as a series of positions. The series comprises ethnographic vignettes, composing a kind of cultural account of stereotypes in some contemporary anthropology. Each position and counter position is presented as though it were composed of position and counter position (counter position in the sense of being apposite, not necessarily an opposite). The structure is artificially 'self-scaling.' To follow the initial breaks, a depiction of ethnography as evocation jumps to a depiction of the contemporary world as cosmopolitan, polyphonic, multi-cultured; the way these two positions turn on a single preoccupation with aesthetics and rhetoric generates a challenge from scholars concerned with the structure of power and interests; feminist scholarship and comparative anthropology provide examples of such positions that are also counter positions to each other, and so forth. Each juxtaposition is generated out of thoughts left over from a previous position.

For the human subject, of course, such as the reader of the text, to be able to look both backward and forward from these positions may well make the gaps seem like ground traversed, a journey taken. Certainly, the metaphor of journeying is as culturally salient these days for all kinds of intellectual activity as pictures of chaos might well become. The writer, though, is defeated by the illusory sense of artifice — for in truth one also finds, uncannily, the same issues and arguments recurring unexpectedly, and barely under the control of conscious anticipation. Perhaps that sense of *déjà vu* is also a sense of habitation within a cultural matrix.

*　　　*　　　*　　　*　　　*　　　*

Self-proclaimed artifice can be intensely irritating. It looks as though complexity is being produced for its own sake. How much more satisfying for the reader or commentator to be able to uncover the artifice for her or himself! Indeed, this is what anthropologists 'do' in their analysis of the accounts other peoples give of themselves, and it has recently become a source of satisfaction in the scrutiny of earlier anthropological accounts to display their realism for the artifice it conceals.

The present exercise is grounded in commonplace and real enough problems that constantly recur in the anthropological organization of cultural materials. My obvious hope is that these awkward and persistent issues will seem culturally interesting phenomena. I can only re-ground them by further hoping that you will uncover something beyond the artifice — perhaps in unlooked-for connections that disturb the arrangement of the account I have given and for which I have therefore given no account. They would point to the gaps in it.

This preface will introduce a perturbation of sorts. "Writing Anthropology" is the book, its title *Partial Connections*, with "Writing Anthropology" the second "title" that talked about the book before it diverged into roughly equal sections, ending up with "Writing Anthropology" as the subtitle of the very last subsection. But the bifurcations were always uneven, and perhaps a subsidiary set of "Partial Connections" is an opportunity to reflect on how the volume took the form it does, why it might still be of interest, and indeed why it might be best preserved in its own time frame of the late 1980s; the text is reproduced here unmodified.

Behind the play was a purpose. For some while I had been overcome by the notion that it was not insufficient materials that posed a problem for anthropology, but amplitude. I said as much in the opening pages of *The Gender of the Gift* (1988). Yet the mild comments there did not do justice to my sense not just of amplitude but excess, although that subsequently found its way into a query about getting rid of unwanted images (1999: 45–6; cf. Munro 1992). It was the time when it seemed that scholars and universities alike were going to have to double the information they produced—not only carrying out research but also adding layers of description about themselves and their research activities as part of an academic performance for auditing purposes. The being done and the performance of researching were not commensurate. No surprise that information overload seemed a new burden, but possibly a surprise that it may have fueled a new perception that answers had to lie not in the adding of data but in reducing it. Yet in relation to data, or in relation to interpretation, for that matter, where can the perception of excess possibly come from? There will be many routes to answering this question: one includes pointing to the ways in which crises of confidence of the kind generated by audit and new practices of accountability—and mirrored in internal reflexivity—lead practitioners to look beyond the boundaries of existing fields and thus create new incommensurables. But then, some would say that excess has always lain at the heart of interpretative practice.

Interpretation must be a matter of refusing many meanings in order to focus on any. Weiner (1995: 5, original emphasis) develops the point from a comment that a famous Yolngu artist, Naritjin, said to Howard Morphy. "Faced with the task of interpreting the work of art, Naritjin chose to explain to Morphy that it was a matter of *refusing* meanings their purchase on our imagination, rather than devising structures within which they can proliferate." Yet this quasi-quantification is itself elusive. Weiner adds that the social efficacy and power of artistic practices cannot be measured simply because there are no discrete units of meaning. At the same time, there are certainly practices of interpretation, in which one might include the anthropological exercise, that rest on an explicit desire to *match* the effort under study with effort at understanding. It is raised, mundanely, every time someone asks how sufficient an interpretation seems. In an analytical project, insufficiency might appear as the underdetermination of solutions. So there is always "more" data that needs to be brought in or "more" effort at interpretation or analysis required. The analytical problems we thus present ourselves with can seem not up to, equal to, the quantity or complexity of the data at our disposal—or, conversely, data might not seem adequate to theoretical ambition. This is the issue pursued in *Partial Connections*.

*   *   *   *   *   *

For me, there was a very practical dimension to this. I finished *GOG*, an exercise of synthesis (and therefore with some pretensions to an overview) in the midst of work still streaming out of Melanesia and out of feminist writings; I therefore set myself the bibliographical limit of 1985. But while I was still writing, materials were piling up and demanding attention, not least "Writing Culture" (Clifford and Marcus 1986). In responding to two invitations (they came in 1987 and 1988) that prompted my first assay at *Partial Connections*, I set myself a further bibliographical focus—1987—although one or two references subsequently strayed into 1988 or 1989. It was the year Gleick's popularizer on chaos theory appeared. I recall thinking that if *GOG* tried to set up a fence of sorts behind which decades of Melanesian and other literature was corralled, *PC* was more like a punctuation, a moment that was "caught" in 1987.

Perhaps there is something here a little more interesting than this play as well. The opening paragraph of *Partial Connections* lays it out: how to match two dimensions of the anthropological exercise in which one invariably relativizes the other, invariably renders one insufficient to the other's amplitude. Matching would entail commensurability to the extent of giving equal weight to each. I had ended *GOG* (e.g. 1988: 329) on the note of mock despair that no equalizing of the writing could shift the disproportionate weights that gender imagery carried in English (to signal gender always seemed to signal an unequal apportioning of importance). This was in large part a matter of the way language tended to veer off in unlooked-for directions, that is, it was a problem with "writing anthropology." And I was quite touchy about the "size" of data. Critics of *GOG* complained that I had not made men (that is, violence) big enough. So what is big or small? The question to be asked of data is also, of course, a question to be asked of societies that anthropologists tend to categorize as "large scale" or "small scale," and for all that they tell themselves otherwise, thereby end up apportioning importance unequally.

Not mock at all was the sense that I had not accomplished a comparative exercise—synthesis had not got rid of the problem of "comparison." *PC* tries to set up a series of instances in which the question about unit of comparison is examined. In the earlier work, several of the ethnographic examples focus on initiation rituals. What precisely is one comparing with what? This was an old question for anthropologists, concerned as they once were with analogies and homologies across cultures. If such rituals are "absent" in (say) Hagen, are they really not there or are they there in some other form? Indeed, what can presence or absence of a trait mean? Should we not be thinking about what is implicit or explicit, or about what is hidden and what is made visible? What gets lost or hidden by moving one's analytical position, for instance? All this seemed to add up to an issue that did seemed worth exploring: scale. Not just judgments about analogy but judgments about proportion inform any organization of data. Now this was the moment that Donna Haraway was introducing the language of the cyborg that permitted "partial" connections. (Partiality only works as a connection: a part by itself is a whole. The Foi men's house described in Weiner [1995:7] is one example; when it divides, each part fills the whole space for occupants). Her semi-machine worked for me more than all the talk, at the time, of collage, montage, fragmentation and the monotone re-discovery of ineffable diversity. Then there was her interest in layering, where subtracting has the same effect as adding—it allows movement. Her vision was much closer to what I had called partibility, neither the fragmentation of the person nor its reflexive recognition through the other, but the *social* logic that makes half of a whole one of pair. Rather than inadvertent or unforeseen—and thus tragic or pitiable—partitionings that conjured loss of a whole, I wanted to experiment with the apportioning of "size" in a deliberate manner.

The strategy was to stop the flow of information or argument, and thus "cut" it. In the text that follows, each section break is a cut, a lacuna: one can see similar themes on either side, but they are not added to one another. My own version of Cantor's Dust was an artificial device to try to make the material in each section (or set of sections, or half of the book) appear consistently sized. Add or subtract, one never reduces complexity. So the size had to be an effect of perception, not of word count. The hope was that in the end the comparative Melanesian excursus would be as "large" as the theoretical excursus, and vice versa. The idea of this artifice was to enable us to see what we do when we are not aware of it.

And what gets left over. No analysis or description is complete: in this book each new section takes off (and arbitrarily) from an element in the previous one. Later, in *After Nature* (1992: 73), I was to develop this effect of Euro-American discursiveness and called it "merographic" (nothing to do with parts and wholes, which would have been mereographic, but a phenomenon that needed a new term, namely the fact that any part of one thing may also be part of something else). It should be added that while one can use the merographic connection to organize Melanesian material, one would be doing so from a Euro-American perspective; it is an organizing feature of Euro-American life, and thus a Euro-American, not a Melanesian, device. So, for Euro-Americans at least, the concept can have some purchase as an analytic tool. By contrast I do not think that "partial connections" says anything more or less than, for example, the phrase "writing anthropology" does. In this book it refers to relations through partition, through cutting out obvious connecting material.

The writing of *PC* thus overlapped with the lectures given in 1989 that led to *After Nature*. They included among other things an investigation of the kind of mathematics that had Westerners / Euro-Americans end up with western "individualism." However, "numerical metaphors" might be a more accurate description than mathematics here. Certainly no mathematical knowledge lay behind my attraction to fractals. The impetus was all from what I knew of the behavior of social relations and of the task of describing them. I add (subtract) here the observation that the exercise undertaken in *Partial Connections* was an attempt to act out, or deliberately fabricate, a non-linear progression of argumentative points as the basis for description.

*   *   *   *   *   *

In his introduction to a volume on *On the Order of Chaos: Social Anthropology and the Science of Chaos* (Mosko and Damon, forthcoming), Mosko points out that anthropologists have occasionally drawn on chaos theory for inspiration, as it has been developed in the natural sciences, but have (in his words) tended to rely on analogies to a few selected parts of the theory. This could not be more true for *PC*. As for the limitations of analogy, one need only contrast my very simple analogizing with Eglash's (1997; cf. 1995) sophisticated use of Cantor's Dust in analyzing Bamana sand divination. Interestingly, Eglash also shows that the very divide between deploying theory and drawing analogies (mathematics and culture is the contrast he uses) replicates itself either side of that divide as well, an analytical phenomenon the introduction here ("Writing Anthropology") also lays out. Antinomies of this kind do not "cut" the date—rather they proliferate in smaller (larger) and smaller (larger) segments of it, and thus across different scales. One instance is evident in the way I have run together analysis, interpretation and theoretical discussion as though they were all partitioned from "data" (or cross-cultural comparison), where clearly analysis and interpretation can both be separated from theorizing, and then analysis separated from interpretation (e.g. van Meter 2003). The phenomenon of interest would be the extent to which similar apprehensions of data, or of operations on data, do the same dividing work each time. And of course at each partition how what was before a subset comes to take up the same amount of space previously occupied by the whole.

Some of the impetus—and much of the groundwork—for Damon and Mosko's own volume dates from a meeting they convened at the American Anthropological Association in 1992. It was clearly prescient in anthropology. (Over at the American Sociological Association that year, O'Brien [1992] was talking about holographic theory and collectivity in culture.) Nonetheless, at the time there were various forays across unexpected divides, of which a few have come my way. For example, in 1989 in the House of Lords, the Archbishop of York used the Mandelbrot set to press home a point about embryo development (Strathern 1992: 144–7). In the early 1990s the mathematician Abraham was tracking down dynamic systems across several disciplines outside the sciences, including economics and the "social sciences" (http://www.ralph-abraham.org/articles, nos. 74, 76, 83). He offered a commentary (1993) on "human fractals" from a mathematician's view, citing Haraway (1985), Eglash and Broadwell (1989) and Wagner (1991). (He also, no doubt inadvertently, has too many references to myself that need to be reduced to two, *Partial Connections* and "One legged gender" [1993].) Later, I wish I had purused references to Caribbean work on chaos supplied by colleagues in Taiwan (Baker 1993; Benítez-Rojo 1997).

But there has been nothing linear about these forays. A decade on, now, and recent editions of the *Annual Reviews in Anthropology* have carried fascinating articles on incommensurability (Povinelli 2001), and on complex adaptive systems (Lansing 2003). Their bibliographies hardly touch the works assembled here—at one or two points at the most.

*   *   *   *   *   *

I owe many thanks to the indulgence of ASAO (Association for Social Anthropology in Oceania), the Special Publications Editor, Lamont Lindstrom and the Association's Chair, Joel Robbins. If the original motivation was problems in "writing anthropology," these extra words have tried to keep true to the original. I have not scaled them up to suggest I was making claims about the human condition or universal cognitive processes or the ineffable in life: these do not need claims made for them. Instead I want to say that it is the small-large tasks we set ourselves that give pleasure. There were all kinds of reasons why I enjoyed what I was doing at the time. I have left the dedication as it was.

Marilyn Strathern
January 2004

REFERENCES

Abraham, Ralph. 1993. Human fractals: the Arabesque in our mind, *Visual Anthropology Review*, 9: 52–55.

Baker, Patrick L. 1993. *Centring the periphery: Chaos, order, and the ethnohistory of Dominica*, Montreal: McGill-Queen's University Press.

Benítez-Rojo, Antonio. 1997. *The repeating island: The Caribbean and the postmodern perspective*. Durham: Duke University Press.

Eglash, Ron. 1995. Fractal geometry in African material culture, *Symmetry: Culture and Science*, 6: 174–77.

Eglash, Ron. 1997. Bamana Sand divination: Recursion in ethnomathematics, *American Anthropologist* 99 (1), 112–122.

Eglash, Ron, and P. Broadwell. 1989. Fractal geometry in traditional African architecture, *Dynamics Newsletter* 3 (4): 4–9.

Lansing, J. Stephen. 2003. Complex adaptive systems, *Annual Review of Anthropology*, 32: 183–294.

Mosko, Mark and Fred Damon, (eds). Forthcoming. *On the Order of Chaos: Social Anthropology and the Science of Chaos*. New York: Berghahn Press, In press.

Munro, Rolland. 1995. *Disposal of the body: Upending postmodernism.* Proceedings of the Standing Conference on Organizational Symbolism, University of Lancaster.

O'Brien, John D. 1992. "The reality of cultural integration: A constrained holographic theory of collectivity in culture." Paper presented to the American Sociological Association, Pittsburgh.

Povinelli, Elizabeth A. 2001. Radical worlds: The anthropology of incommensurability and inconceivability, *Annual Review of Anthropology*, 30: 319–34.

Strathern, Marilyn. 1988. *The Gender of the Gift: Problems with women and problems with society in Melanesia*. Berkeley and Los Angeles: University of California Press.

Strathern, Marilyn. 1992. "A partitioned process," in *Reproducing the future: Anthropology, kinship and the new reproductive technologies*. Manchester: Manchester University Press.

Strathern, Marilyn. 1993. One-legged gender, *Visual Anthropology Review*, 9: 42–51.

Strathern, Marilyn. 1999. The aesthetics of substance, in *Property, substance and effect: Anthropological essays on persons and things*. London: Athlone Press.

van Meter, Karl (ed). 2003. *Interrelation between type of analysis and type of interpretation*. Bern: Peter Lang.

Weiner, James (ed). 1995. "Too many meanings; A critique of the anthropology of aesthetics," *Social Analysis* 38 (special Issue).

ACKNOWLEDGEMENTS

Two occasions stimulated me to write the paper on which the following is based. The first was an invitation from the Department of Social Anthropology at Edinburgh University to speak in the 1987 Munro Lecture series. The second was an invitation from the Association of Social Anthropology in Oceania to give the annual Distinguished Lecture for 1988. On both occasions my sponsors were lavish in their hospitality, and I warmly thank Eric Hanley and his colleagues at Edinburgh, and the A.S.A.O in the person of the then Chair, Terence Hays.

The suggestion that the lecture might be brought out as an A.S.A.O. publication came from Deborah Gewertz, and it is largely due to her patience, encouragement and substantive commentary that it appears at all. She has also been as meticulous as an editor as Jean Ashton has been in preparing the typescript. I express my considerable gratitude. As I do to critics, several of whom were certainly irritated by the initial version — apparently discursive but in fact non-expository and full of lacuna or, worse, a series of private connections with all the randomness of a personal trajectory. I have tried not to argue these faults away. My thanks remain, to those and to others for their commentaries: Anthony Cohen, Johannes Fabian, Richard Fardon, Lisette Josephides, Nigel Rapport, James Weiner. I also appreciate the insights of Alan Barnard, Donna Haraway, Aihwa Ong, Margaret Rodman, Jukka Siikala, Judith Stacey, Stephen Tyler. Some, but not all, of the comments on which I draw are indicated in the text as "pers. comm."; I am grateful for individual permissions to cite unpublished work ("n.d."). Claudia Gross, at the University of Manchester, has since been a helpful and perceptive critic of the longer manuscript.

There is a further history to the present form of this monograph. On hearing the first version, Roy Wagner recast one of my 'partial connections' in terms of a mathematical image (see 'The Fractal Person,' in press). It was a powerful provocation. I have exploited a dimension of the idea here — a quite shameless appropriation, but a shamelessness that is not so culturally inappropriate for our times. There is no apprehension of mathematics on my part, but the imagery for its part grabs me.

Margaret Willson at the London School of Economics subsequently showed me some of the plates from Gleick's book on **Chaos** (first published in 1987) when it was on the verge of becoming a bestseller: my thanks for her anticipation.

Permission for the reproduction of plates and figures is gratefully acknowledged: The Frontispiece to Part One is an illustration from Page 93 of James Gleick's, **Chaos: Making a New Science,** published by Viking Penguin Inc., New York; the illustration initially appeared in **The Fractal Geometry of Nature** by Benoit B. Mandelbrot, Copyright (c) 1977, 1982, 1983 and is reproduced with permission from W. H. Freeman and Company. The Frontispiece to Part Two and Figure 1 are illustrations from pages 70, 122, 123 of Carl A. Schmiotz, **Wantoat: Art and Religion of the Northeast New Guinea Papuans** reproduced with permission from Mouton de Gruyter, Berlin, and from Frau Martha Schmitz.

Manchester   <u>Marilyn Strathern</u>
                                                    September 1987
                                                    September 1989

I. WRITING ANTHROPOLOGY

A Geometry of Nature

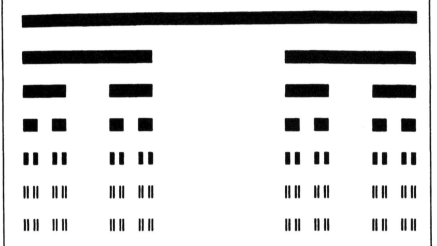

THE CANTOR DUST. Begin with a line; remove the middle third; then remove the middle third of the remaining segments; and so on. The Cantor set is the dust of points that remains. They are infinitely many, but their total length is 0.

The paradoxical qualities of such constructions disturbed nineteenth-century mathematicians, but Mandelbrot saw the Cantor set as a model for the occurrence of errors in an electronic transmission line. Engineers saw periods of error-free transmission, mixed with periods when errors would come in bursts. Looked at more closely, the bursts, too, contained error-free periods within them. And so on—it was an example of fractal time. At every time scale, from hours to seconds, Mandelbrot discovered that the relationship of errors to clean transmission remained constant. Such dusts, he contended, are indispensable in modeling intermittency.

An illustration from James Gleick's **Chaos: Making a New Science.**

P.1.   A E S T H E T I C S

P.1.   ETHNOGRAPHY AS EVOCATION

P.1. EVOCATION

P.1. Representation and Evocation. An ethnographic account is conventionally the description of a particular society and culture known to be based at some point on the experiences and observations of a fieldworker 'who was there'. In the past such accounts have been taken as representations of the way societies and cultures are organized, thus providing objects for analysis and theory. But anthropologists are currently much preoccupied with the nature of representation as such; Stephen Tyler, whose image of ethnography as evocation I take as my starting point, defines what he means by opposing evocation to representation. The opposition is no accident: it is echoed in other academic disciplines. What has become problematized, in the words of one, is the very activity of reference itself.[11]

Anthropologists' preoccupations take a typical two-forked turn. They argue about how to interpret the meaning of the actions, artefacts, words and so on produced by the people they study, understood as values and qualities that people thereby represent to themselves. Simultaneously they argue about how the ethnographer represents these meanings in the art of writing. The very activity of 'representation' is further queried in the current critique that no more nor less than the people he or she studies can the ethnographer occupy a position outside his or her productions. Writing is much more, in this view, than the recording of facts and observations. Consequently, the ethnographer can no longer pretend to be a neutral vector for the conveying of information; her or his own participation in the constructed narrative must be made explicit. Anthropological narratives, it is argued, do not refer to an independent reality which can be grasped by other means but create that sense of reality in the act of narration. The only way that reality can be grasped, then, is through a medium that already has a form of its own. To be true to the nature of human interlocution, especially the interlocutionary process of fieldwork, the writer/ ethnographer must invite the reader in turn to participate in what s/he participates, which is discourse.

Rather than simply adding to such criticism, Tyler does something much more effective. He provides a recipe for how anthropologists must understand what ethnography does. His starting point is that "the point of discourse is not how to make a better representation, but how to avoid representation" (1986:128). Ethnography works, Tyler suggests, by evoking in the reader responses that cannot be commensurate with the writer's — there is no 'object' that they both grasp, for the writer cannot 'represent' another society or culture; rather s/he provides the reader with a connection to it. Ethnography makes available what can be conceived but not presented. The connection is perceptible as the reader's realization of an experience (what the ethnographer has evoked for him or her). "Since evocation is nonrepresentational, it is not to be understood as a sign function, for it is not a 'symbol of', nor does it 'symbolize' what it evokes . . . Ethnographic discourse is itself neither an object to be represented nor a representation of an object" (Tyler 1986:129, 131). Whereas many of the critiques lead to prescriptions about the form that ethnographies should take if they are to make explicit the interlocutionary process of their production, Tyler's reconceptualization would apply to any form. It is the response to ethnographies he wishes to alter.

Tyler gives us in turn an arresting ethnography of our times. He provides an exemplar of what it would be like if we were to really engage in the contemporary developments to which so many — and I include myself — are merely content to make reference. I say contemporary to capture his self-conscious postmodernism. Tyler's claims for anthropology are based on conceptualizing evocation as "the discourse of the post-modern world" (1986:123), with ethnography its quintessential form. That world, he says, has lost the vision of scientific enquiry leading to a unity of knowledge.

Of all aspects of anthropological endeavor, however, Tyler's reconceptualization of ethnography, his closeting of reader and writer, would seem to have no place for comparative analysis. Comparative analysis was once anthropology's claim to distinction within the social sciences. As Ladislav Holy (1987) puts it, both generalization about human behavior and the facility to translate cultures have in the past depended upon cross-societal comparison. Yet it sounds as though the denial that the ethnographer is representing the facts or providing objects of knowledge would be quite undermining of either procedure. How can one embark on comparison if the purpose of ethnography is evocation? Comparing evocations is not inconceivable (Nigel Rapport, pers. comm.) but it would be, of course, for their resonances and effects, in short for their aesthetic impact.

In fact, as Holy makes clear, conventional comparative methods are themselves at a current impasse. Here Tyler has provided a new point of departure. We need a new position because, whether we like it or not, we cannot recapture past ones.

P.2. Aesthetic Impasse.   The current critique that has become general in much anthropological thinking, commonly dubbed reflexive, draws its own position from past ones. Principally, it makes a problem out of what was once unproblematic: the figure of the fieldworker. The person who 'went into' the field and then returned to translate her or his observations into an authentic representation of the 'culture' or 'society' no longer convinces. The authority of having been there turns out to be no authority, but a pre-emption of authorship. Not only did the anthropologist take this role on her or himself in a quite unauthorized sense, but concealed the process by which s/he arrived at the final description in the interest of self-generating theoretical preoccupations.

No one is suggesting that anthropologists should stop fieldwork. Rather, the problems surround the kind of narratives they produce — hence the solutions appear to do with how one writes. What is discredited, in other words, is the elision between fieldworker, writer and author. The kind of author one should be, it is argued nowadays, has to be settled in terms of the relationships established in the field, the audiences one wishes to reach, the messages at stake. It cannot be settled by the authority of the fieldworker who was there.

But that lone figure from the past was quite a complex character. Cooperative ventures and teamwork aside, the fieldworker was typically one person. Yet her head, or his head, became the locus for the gathering together of diverse materials. Fieldworkers sometimes presented themselves as learning the cultural ground rules, their task to know how to act as a member of that society. However, they did not mean that they replicated the knowledge of a particular person. What they meant was that they learnt how it might be to be any member. In other words, the fieldworker came to know 'more' than his or her informants, so-called, and that generalized information about what was common to many informants could be aggregated as the culture of these people.

So the ethnographer/anthropologist[12] simultaneously enjoyed a one-to-one relationship with each informant, and enjoyed a one-to-one relationship with the whole culture. The capacity to describe an entire system lay in the capacity to synthesize a disparate range of facts. To cast the allegory in personal terms: in relation to my first field area, Hagen in the Papua New Guinea Highlands, I can connect domestic organization to politics, as I can speak of the systemic relationship between ideas about clanship and the exchange of women in marriage. I do not take an organic metaphor of a society as body literally, any more than I do the mechanical metaphor of structures and systems with their ratchet-like transmissions of effects, but I **am** likely to treat these metaphors as indicating the potential integration of everything under study. Integration also appears possible because in making everything come together, as in monologue, I imagine myself as a singular person.

The single scholar did not replicate the diverse experiences of another single person, then, but encompassed within her or his person what went on between diverse people — **their** interrelations — as an object of reflection (their society/culture). S/he could imagine this object as connections between persons otherwise like the scholar except in being able to envision the connections as such. The observer's vision was a holistic, unifying assumption about the integration of meaning. Cross-cultural comparison then proceeded as a higher order integration — either connections between societies or between independent variables across many societies — and on the basis of communication with other scholars, persons otherwise alike except in being able to share the uniqueness of their own experiences.

Other anthropologists could see the connections, but not claim that experience; each was presumed to speak, however, on the authority of their own one-to-one relationships. There was, I suggest, a potential elision between the individual person of the fieldworker and the specific culture s/he described, and between the imagined integration of a society as a collectivity of persons and the integrating efforts (the external 'mind') of anthropologists at large.

The singular and holistic fieldworker/anthropologist thus managed both internal and external connections, and for a long while this figure worked as an aesthetic form. 'The fieldworker' was a powerful portrayal of the single consumer or receptor of experience: the ability to even speak about a range of phenomena implicitly guaranteed integration at some level. (You knew there were connections because one person was making them.) I say aesthetic because I refer to the persuasiveness of form, the elicitation of a sense of appropriateness.

The emergent critique that focuses on the authority of the fieldworker can be seen as a residue of postcolonial anguish, though it is not only focused on exposing hidden power relations between anthropologist and informant. Nor for that matter does it simply envisage a clearer perception of the messiness and inconsequentiality of everyday life, or of engineering through fiction and illusion a closer approximation than the orthodox monograph to the half-heard resonances of what people have half-meant. Of course, anguish can never be adequate to the power relations involved, any more than a confused text is equal to the confusions of life. The whole point is that representation has come to be perceived as an insufficiency. The nub of current reflection thus lies in its self-evident emergence: our efforts do not carry the conviction they once did. There has been a shift.

An image loses its power the moment it becomes a subject for argument, as a paradigm is revealed at the moment it ceases to be taken for granted. And since images do not survive debate, to box with an image does have an air of unreality to it. This has been the discovery of those contemporary critics who are trying to re-direct our sense of what ethnography is about. In demolishing the figure of the single fieldworker as a single voice, and implanting the idea of an ethnography as a composition of many, the new critics appear to be obsessed only with literary issues, their work dismissable as "self-congratulatory, narcissistic decadence" (Sangren 1988:423).

The charge of self-indulgence hardly gets to the heart of the matter. Lisette Josephides (n.d.) summarizes the shift as being from a position where the monograph is treated as a unique and visionary work, informative about its subject matter, to a text treated as already written, to be understood allegorically.[13] In other words, works are judged as texts in terms of their impact. Reflexive critique is centrally preoccupied with the character of impact or effect.

So anthropologists find themselves in a new aesthetic. Or rather, the single figure is displaced by the figure of the reflexivist in debate. Concomitantly, the 'single author' is no longer an image of authenticity, the 'one culture' or 'one society' no longer valid as a unit of study. This change is not open to adjudication. There are no rights and wrongs to weigh up, but something that was right has become wrong, in the sense that what once persuaded no longer can. A form that once worked to create an authentic effect no longer does so.

P.2. JOURNEY

P.1. The Anti-aesthetic Break. I was tempted into considering the single fieldworker as an aesthetic form by the nature of current critiques. I return to Tyler's essay as both belonging to and going beyond much prevalent commentary.

One criticism is that anthropologists must make explicit the participatory nature of fieldwork. A postmodern ethnography, Tyler agrees, must be seen as a "cooperatively evolved text consisting of fragments of discourse intended to evoke in the minds of both reader and writer an emergent fantasy of a possible world of commonsense reality" (1986:125). The participation of writer and reader, corresponding to participation of fieldworker and informant in the original creation of the text, "rejects the ideology of 'observer-observed' . . . There is instead the mutual, dialogical production of a discourse, of a story of sorts" (1986:126). In lieu of the one author/fieldworker, then, we have the polyphony of many voices, either based on the reciprocities of fieldwork or else brought to light as hidden alternatives when a text is read as an allegory and the allegory of ethnographic practice as textualization is revealed (Clifford 1986). Multiple authorship convinces the reader of a different kind of authenticity: what it is to be a participant in the composition. The reader is made aware of her or his re-working of an artefact, for in this view the ideal polyphonic text has in itself no final form or encompassing synthesis. Multiplicity or variability is taken as a challenge to form. (Ethnography "evokes what can never be put into a text" (Tyler 1986:138).)

This new invitation to awareness has similarities to an anti-aestheticism claimed elsewhere. In his introduction to a collection of essays quixotically called **Postmodern Culture,** Hal Foster (1985:xv, original emphasis) remarks:

> the rubric 'anti-aesthetic'. . . . is **not** intended as one more
> assertion of the negation of art or of representation as
> such. It was modernism that was marked by such 'ne-
> gations',. . . . the utopian dream of a time of pure present,
> a space beyond representation. This is not the case here:
> all these critics take for granted that we are never outside

> representation — or rather, never outside its politics.
> Here then, 'anti-aesthetic' is the sign not of a modern
> nihilism . . . but rather of a critique which destructures
> the order of representations in order to reinscribe them.

The anthropological counterpart to the modernists' 'pure' aesthetic form
was never the ethnography: it was the 'culture'/'society' itself, about which
the anthropologist anonymously wrote.[14] So for the anthropologist to discover
'ethnography' in its marked sense, to discover her or his own place in
these representations, is tantamount to breaking up what was before seen
as a whole. The postmoderns' polyphonic text is anti-aesthetic in Foster's
(1985:xv) specific sense.

> [Fredric Jameson considers] why classical modernism is
> a thing of the past and why post-modernism should have
> taken its place. Th[e] new component is what is generally
> called 'the death of a subject' or, to say it in more
> conventional language, the end of individualism as such.
> The great modernisms were . . . predicated on the invention
> of a personal, private style, as unmistakable as your
> fingerprint, as incomparable as your own body. But this
> means that the modernist aesthetic is in some way or-
> ganically linked to the conception of a unique self and
> private identity . . . which can be expected to generate
> its own unique vision of the world and to forge its own
> unique, unmistakable style. (1985:114)

If modernism in art was predicated on personal, private styles, and its
counterpart in anthropology was the fieldworkers' rendering of other people's
authentic and unique cultures, each with its unmistakable style,[15] then the
'death of a fieldworker' has been necessary to the break.

Paul Rabinow underlines the connection Jameson makes with the break-
down of interest in the relationship between signifiers. The death of a
subject means the death of perspective, of the perceiving organism which
orients itself to a world beyond itself and to which its ideas refer. Yet once
"the signifier is freed from a concern with its relation to an external referent
it does not float free of any referentiality at all; rather, its referent becomes
other texts, other images" (Rabinow 1986:250). Hence Jameson's (1985:115)
famous prescription.

> once again, pastiche: in a world in which stylistic inno-
> vation is no longer possible, all that is left is to imitate
> dead styles, to speak through the masks and with the
> voices of the styles in the imaginary museum.

For the modernist sense of the uniqueness and thus plurality of each culture, postmoderns must substitute cultures that can only be apprehended as versions of other cultures. It becomes apparent that anthropologists have been using the languages and images of some to evoke others (Boon 1982). Juxtaposing cultures and societies makes them into imitations, echoes of one another, as their social forms echo the descent groups or marriage alliances or stratification systems that were 'first' described elsewhere (cf. Appadurai 1986; Marcus 1988). Thus particular ethnographic regions have stamped their resonating style on the anthropological description of certain phenomena such as caste or gift exchange (Fardon 1990). Stylistic innovation seems no longer possible because the anthropologist has realized he or she can only speak about cultures through cultures, about kinship in the New Guinea Highlands through African systems of kinship and marriage. What is new is the realization.

This seems to imply that the original scaffolding of comparative analysis has been dismantled. To consider such various analytical constructs for the way they were deployed in this or that monograph and for how they have been introduced elsewhere turns each wave of monographs into a commentary upon other monographs. Descent or caste or the gift are no longer 'seen' as the autonomous constructs which allowed anthropologists to compare their phenomenal manifestation in a plurality of situations. The purpose of comparison disappears: all that exists is the internal referencing of one anthropological text to another, and there the permutations are endless.

Such is the impression that Tyler's self-location within a postmodern anti-aesthetic also gives. But there is more to Tyler's invitation as to how we should approach ethnography, and an invitation that does not, all the same, take us quite far enough.

P.2. A Hidden Form. One literary/anthropological model for a polyphonic text is Crapanzano's (1985) book on whites in South Africa. It eschews direct comparison of the different phenomena he describes, avoids deliberate framing or encompassing. The book is held together by the device of juxtaposition. He sets side by side diverse encounters with inhabitants from a small settlement outside Cape Town, their accounts a composite of topics, issues, themes. It is also a composite of the different 'societies' of the South African polity. Is this the sociological analog to pastiche, image following image with only the sedimentation of previous evocation connecting the one with the other in the reader's mind?[16] But there is another dimension to the account. As he says at the beginning, "I have accompanied those stories with my own" (Crapanzano 1985:xiii).

Crapanzano's book deals with the effects of the political situation upon himself, and thus the way they turn back on his own circumstances. And

Tyler would **not** be content with a simple succession of positions, or the superimposition of one upon another, with the only connections between them being hints, echoes and reminders of other positions which may or may not be present — the trick of collage that "consists also of never entirely suppressing the alterity of . . . elements reunited in a temporary composition".

> Every sign, linguistic or non-linguistic, spoken or written
> (in the current sense of this opposition), in a small or
> large unit, can be **cited**, put between quotation marks;
> in so doing it can break with every given context,
> engendering an infinity of new contexts in a manner
> which is absolutely illimitable (Derrida, quoted by Ulmer
> 1985:88, original emphasis).[17]

In fact, Tyler dissociates himself from such illimitability. For he denies that the postmodernism of ethnography is defined by its form — pastiche or not, there is no predetermined form. Hence his impatience with the idea of representation. Rather, Tyler suggests, in its evocatory capacity all ethnography has a postmodern character.[18] Evocation means that reading an ethnography must be understood as a process of departure **and return**.

Thus ethnographic evocation can be imagined as therapy, as he puts it, healing the alienating breach between self and other, subject and object, language and the world. Anti-aesthetic with regards to form, postmodern ethnography is nevertheless a return to an idea of integration. "Post-modern ethnography is an object of meditation that provokes a rupture with the commonsense world and evokes an **aesthetic integration** whose therapeutic effect is worked out in the **restoration** of the commonsense world. . . [I]t does not hold out the false hope of a permanent, utopian transcendence, which can only be achieved by devaluing and falsifying the commonsense world . . . Instead it departs from the commonsense world only in order to reconfirm it and return us to it renewed and mindful of our renewal" (1986:134, my emphasis). Tyler does not invite us to imagine an illimitable array of experiences or contexts: he imagins a recursive activity which returns writer and reader to their own worlds. What is at once ethnography's realism and its fantasy is its capacity to intimate "a possible world already given to us in fantasy and commonsense, those foundations of our knowledge that cannot themselves be the objects of our knowledge" (Tyler 1986:134).

If I understand him, then, Tyler is breaking in turn with the image of pastiche or collage, in order to substitute the sense of recursive, substitutive positioning implied in the image of departure and return. But the manner in which he so presents it falls short. He cannot, I think, make his cognitive utopia of author-text-reader as "an emergent mind that has no individual locus" (1986:133) do all the work that it needs to do if that sense of positioning is to persuade. It is an insufficient tool for the purpose. Let me try to say why.

Tyler is concerned with how ethnography reworks what is already known, with its impact, both in the writing and the reading of it, on previous experience. But while he joins with others to demolish the figure of the single fieldworker/author, he does not demolish the integration of the ethnographic experience: however momentary, that remains integrating **in its effect** ("a new kind of holism"). And that effect is registered in the person of the writer/reader. Remember that in his terms it is not the form that we are concerned with but the nature of the ethnography's elicitory capacity. For the effects of therapeutic integration to be shown, they must be registered in someone; if a journey is to be taken, there must be one who takes the journey. ("The break with everyday reality is a journey" which disorients "the quester's" consciousness but finally casts him or her "up onto the familiar, but forever transformed, shores of the commonplace world" (1986:126).) Ethnographic rupture is imagined as the dislocation of place and time, as they **happen to** a traveller.

There is a hidden aesthetic form here, and it is that of the deconstructing journey, the anthropologist as tourist indeed (Crick 1985). Writing or reading ethnography is an adventure that leaves one where one began, but perceiving one's location differently because the adventure took place. The juxtaposed experiences of the traveller do not give her or him the long perspective that the observer has on the 'observed'. Rather, they occur in a sequence that always lands the traveller at the end at a different starting point — a round house forever changes one eye for Tudorbethan gables or granite blocks; Frazer 'after' Malinowski (Tyler and Marcus 1987). But whatever her or his encounter with others, the quester's internal transformation is crucial. It is the traveller in whom the experiences of these locations are juxtaposed who becomes renewed. There is an affinity here with the postmodern in whose gaze the collage appears a composition. Indeed, it looks as though the subject has been reborn in the consumer — not with respect to the authorship or even the form of an encounter, but where we imagine its effects take place. Has one killed off the fieldworker, then, only to discover the tourist? Is it not polyphony after all that is at issue but the internal heterogeneity of the aesthete's tastes, the one who selects experiences according to how they work for him or herself? Do we really turn aside from thinking about ourselves as the producers of particular texts only to encounter the voracious consumer of all of them?

If so, this seems an unduly impoverished way to think about departure and return: for the consumer's gut, alas, in the long run turns everything to flesh. Of course, no claims are being made for a whole experience — what is described is the perpetual transformation of experiences, no one encounter substituting entirely for another. Nevertheless, the image returns us to the act of consumption which submits everything to consumerability, each event or observation being equally absorbed in that unifying pastiche, the capacity to experience.

The aesthete's gaze, the tourist's exotic itinerary, have almost nothing to say about the act of consumption itself, about how and where it takes place. What is in the eye or under the feet is already, so to speak, consumed; it is already a 'part of' the consuming body. We have re-discovered that there is no experience outside experience!

Yet 'experience' is also written about, reconstructed, in a specific way. It requires other ideas. Thus, the idea of experience having an integrating effect seems to require an idea of a self. Tyler writes (1986:135, my emphasis) that postmodern ethnography

> aims not to foster the growth of knowledge but to restructure experience; not to understand objective reality, for that is already established by common sense, nor to explain how we understand, for that is impossible, but to reassimilate, **to reintegrate the self in society** and to restructure the conduct of everyday life.

The 'self' appears the subject of therapy, not society. Moreover, the self is finite insofar as society somehow lies beyond. So there are two ideas conjoined here. One, the integrating process turns on its own image: the possibility of a single person realizing a diversity of experiences. But, two, the image falls short of encompassing what the person **also knows**: that his or her experiences are not equal to the diversity of experiences possible. Although the 'integration' of the traveller-tourist's journey takes place within what is perceived as a single body (the self), the body is apparently aware that there are things that lie beyond what it can consume for itself. It touches on these things in its awareness, but does not otherwise turn them to use; they remain external reference points. However briefly, Tyler has to make mention of the self as located in 'society'.

P.2.   COMPLEX SOCIETY, INCOMPLETE KNOWLEDGE

P.1. RETURNED

P.1. Complex Pasts. The set of critiques ('the reflexive turn') that I have summoned as a background to Tyler's specific positioning both has a specific theoretical origin and forms a background to the works of many anthropologists in the 1980s. Yet this is to distinguish figure from ground too clearly. One characteristic of the present arguments is the way the problems the critiques have addressed have become attached to the critiques as their problems.

It is interesting, for instance, that as soon as James Clifford and George Marcus's collection **Writing Culture** (1986) appeared, with its own criticisms and counter-criticisms, it became an example of text-obsessed, literary-derived theorizing. A 'literary turn' then becomes an exemplar of 'the reflexive turn' (cf. Sangren 1988). This is despite the fact that the Introduction comments on the instability of literature and how the literary effects of writing come to be observed,[19] and despite the fact that it deliberately moves from text to discourse, and thus to the socio-historical situating of the ethnographer. The book's critique of representation somehow becomes an exemplar: its concerns are recast in terms of what it criticizes.[20] Perhaps this is the fate of boundary crossers. The loss of master narratives, Josephides observes (n.d.), has complementary effects: Craig Owens's (1985:65) reminder that for literature the loss of narrative is equivalent to the inability to situate oneself historically encounters an anthropology where reproduction of the dialogical bases of narrative composition is thought to add a historical dimension.

An intriguing feature of the present epoch is that similar features can be claimed for both modernism and postmodernism. Jameson (1985:123) puts it strongly: "everything we have described here [pastiche etc.] can be found in earlier periods and most notably within modernism proper"; the difference is that they have become "central features of cultural production". So perhaps one should never have read Tyler as suggesting an 'opposition' between representation and evocation. Rather he makes the one a presence summoned by the other: evocation is to be understood as neither presentation nor representation. But this means in turn that representation is not recovered in any sufficient or complete sense. It is superseded.

But what has been superseded? Anthropology's past seems littered with texts that do not fit comfortably into the realist/representational mold. James Boon (1986) recalls the pactiche of **Tristes Tropiques,** as Clifford (1988:Ch. 4; originally 1981) draws attention to an older surrealist moment in ethnography. Johannes Fabian (n.d.) traces the history of the idea of ethnography itself and the curious disjunction between 'ethnography' and 'writing' that preceded their rapprochement. In any case, what kind of 'modernist text' could Raymond Firth's **The Work of the Gods in Tikopia** in fact illustrate? Did we not always know that descriptions of the Tallensi and Nuer were mediated by anthropological schools of thought and the writings of predecessors and colleagues? And is not the image of the classical single fieldworker a simple back projection?[21]

There appears an incommensurability, then, between the forcefulness of present critiques (critiques and counter critiques) and how they deal with the past. That present concerns should shape past worlds can cause no surprise. But it is hard to shake free of the double telescoping effect — that either the past looks infinitely complex by comparison with the impoverished interpretations of present day concerns; or current subtleties and reflections look infinitely more complex than the straightforward works of one's predecessors. This oscillation is not amenable to arbitration. It is a double bind, for in complexifying the past, as the first position would have it, one necessarily further complexifies the sense of current sensibilities (made aware of and encompassing the past) as the second position would have it.

There can in this sense be no return to the past. Certainly it is to be asked whether one can ever return as a native.[22] But here we encounter the same double effect. For one might equally argue that the difficulty for the traveller is that he or she never really leaves home, however long the journey.[23] In what sense, then, would Tyler return the reader to his or her own world as at once reconfirmed and renewed? What kind of integration awaits the traveller's 'self' when he/she gets back home? What 'society' is there to embrace her or him? He intimates that this consists in the commonsense world, in the conduct of everyday life and quotidian experience (Tyler 1986:135-6).

P.2. Cosmopolitans. There is, however, one contemporary figure that manages to hold together a kind of double complexity, that makes the subtleties of the past a measure for the present — or of other places for the home base — and that is the cosmopolitan. The term I borrow from Rabinow (1986) but use to different effect. I mean to refer to a self-conscious creolization[24] of disciplinary skills or scholarly habitats, to the manner in which present-day writers reveal the complexity of their apprehension of the world through showing the complexities of the past, a mode that finds sufficiency not in reference to just one past figure but in the interweaving of references to many. The cosmopolitan is more than the consumer, then, and more than the tourist, for she or he works to keep active this sense of complexity in claiming it as a source of personal and professional identity.

Ulf Hannerz (1990) presents cosmopolitanism as a perspective or a mode in the 'management of meaning'. In his rendering, cosmopolitan engagements evince a kind of plural cultural competence. More than other travellers, cosmopolitans remain so after return home, for they sustain their diverse orientations elsewhere and hence their personal autonomy from their own culture. Hannerz speaks of a world culture: people make meaning for themselves out of the increasing interconnectedness of local cultures and the development of transnational networks that need no territorial anchorage. He quotes a Hungarian author to the destabilizing effect that international integration nowadays determines universality while national culture has an air of provincialism.

Academic cosmopolitans identify present positions as composites derived from a heterogeneous worldwide constellation of others — figures from anthropology or history or political philosophy — reference to whom always implies further galaxies of 'others'. Neither consumer nor tourist: the differences are not collapsed in the homogeneous gut of the consumer and were not constituted for the sake of the tourist. Diversity is constantly activated, a collage inhabited, so to speak, as so many interruptions that forever take the scholar in different directions. There may well be a self-consciousness about the personal nature of such itineraries, but the landscape is the world.

Yet landscapes too are composed. As Hannerz himself says, people relate to global diversity in different ways. It is not just that they map out different territories, make different discoveries, out of the plurality of times and locations that constitute the cosmos. Forms of pluralism differ. Rapport (n.d.) offers an allegorical contrast between the stereotypes of North American cultural pluralism and British social plurality. In the former, he suggests, ethnic diversity is presented as engendering a democratic sense of cultural difference, the idea that if there is enough cultural difference, then no one set of social interests can dominate. A common denominator is provided by the English language, where shared rules are kept to a minimum and local inventiveness encouraged. By contrast, English in Britain is a language of social exclusion and exclusiveness: 'English' signifies a standard, and thus at once cultural/ethnic singularly and social diversity. Region combines with class to make 'accents' deviate from Received English and susceptible to ranking in relation to it. The moral of the parable is that pluralities have their own configurations.The juxtapositions of food and eating habits one might find in a North American suburb do not necessarily make quite the same cosmopolitans out of their residents that such juxtapositions do in a British suburb. The exclusionary nature of social habits in Britain in any case means that people can be culturally 'of' their society, so to speak, and yet be social misfits wherever they try to live. The itinerant may be a wanderer.[25]

And indeed the countryside 'at home' has always held promise of dangerous journeys. So close to Tyler's commonsense and quotidian world, home is a place where anthropologists never imagined it was possible for the fieldworker to act as 'one person' or claim a single object of study;

where the singular ethnographer was never sufficient to the task, and where unease was always generated about the extent to which fieldwork should be completed by the work of others in other disciplines — local history, political science, social administration. Indeed, the anthropologist's subjects may press home the point, as when Anthony Cohen's (1987:9) Shetlanders convey that whereas once the island of Whalsay was the center of their world, their relation to the periphery beyond has now been inverted — they feel peripheral to a center that must lie elsewhere.

Tyler invokes incompleteness; a postmodern ethnography can never be fully realized because imperfection is the means to its own evocatory or transcendental effect. It is the participating writer/reader, our journeying cosmopolitan, who is momentarily completed on return. But the Western anthropologist studying some aspect of Western society at home faces interruptions of a special kind.

Sociologists, economists, historians — colleagues in other disciplines also interested in the workings of Western society — do not just supply the ethnographer at home with insights or reference points. They are also there as confusing and troubling presences. Indeed one is jostled by the insistence on a presence that is not encompassable by one's own. Evoking them will not 'complete' the anthropological job. They may even seem to get in the way of the task, precisely because they prevent the perception of integration, confounding the image of the fieldworker/anthropologist as a self-sufficient person. What is true for these other voices is also true for the subject of study. Anthropologists often approach the field at home with diffidence. Society appears complex and unmanageable; skills are concentrated, apologetically or defiantly, on specific parts. Another tele-scoping: there seems nothing between such microanthropology and the macroanthropology of grand theory (Hannerz 1986).

In this guise, our cosmopolitan at home seems unable to hold the center together. In any case, if the world is home, and if we believe Jonathan Friedman on the crisis of Western hegemony and shifts in the centers of capital accumulation, we live the "fragmentation of the world system" (1988:427). The production of numerous local cultures, what he calls the ethnicization of Western Europe and America, better suits a dispersed than a transnational image.

A postmodern ethnography, says Tyler (1986:131), is fragmentary because life in the field is fragmentary! Yet perhaps what is imagined as fragmen-tation may be no more derived from a world of fragments than what is imagined as integration comes from a world already a totality. The way the fieldworker at home — in Britain, say — suffers the social presence of others indicates another dimension for the perception of these rela-tionships. The unclosed ear is not simply a telescopic dish scanning the galaxy: people bellow into it; they have claims. They are not standing there juxtaposed — they appear to be connected, rendering the self **available** to constant interruption. Images of neither integration nor fragmentation convey what it feels like to have returned home. Neither trope adequately indicates the nature of presences that impinge.

P.2. PLACED

<u>P.1. Sharing Villages</u>. All the same, various homely and common ways of thinking at first glance endorse a seeming contrast between integration and fragmentation.

It is a commonplace in the sociologized vocabulary of middle class culture that one moves from persona to persona in role playing. This is a vision of the complex society. I am a Melanesianist to this audience, a rural studies person to that; one's 'role' changes as contexts change, and there is nothing remarkable about it. But it is also possible to think about the person as at the center of a constellation of roles, facing in several different directions, the pivot or meeting place for diverse views, the manager at the core of the network. What connects the two suppositions together is the person imagined as an individual. The figure appears either as fragmented **or** as integrated **for the same reason**: because as an individual s/he can always be counterposed to her or his placement, whether 'in' a sociocentric structure or an egocentric network. The individual who gives personal coherence to the network is equally a particle of a structure which defines his or her location. It is intriguing, then, that either position may in turn be seen as a source of personal integration or fragmentation.

Even more intriguing, what I have just described is an English village (M. Strathern 1981). On the one hand English villages are imagined as centers that remain fixed. They form a focus for long-term attachment, containing folk intermeshed in an intricate web of connections, each place a discrete unit looking outwards. On the other hand, they appear to be vanishing institutions. They vanish either because they are left behind, with people moving out to worlds that have nothing to do with the village, or because they are submerged, invaded by people moving in from elsewhere who turn it into a different kind of place, creating a radical fragmentation between a communal then and an anonymous now. The imagined village is replicated in kinship terms — villagers perceive themselves both as the pivot of personal genealogies and as divided into discrete families which can break up and from which they can walk away.

There are connections, then, between certain ideas an English person entertains about individuals who are placed or travel between places, and about places which contain individuals who stay or move, and about the nature of kin ties that are at once mutable and immutable. A person can be a totality or a fragment by either remaining fixed or by being mobile. So when the anthropologist working within 'English' society feels fragmented, then perhaps it is because he or she has the fantasy that only in another place is it possible to be a complete anthropologist with a complete society to study (Cohen 1985:28f). The imaginary figure of the single fieldworker in the simple society returns to haunt the fragmented fieldworker in the complex one.

Commonsense seems to intervene again. From afar, that single figure does appear to work for small 'integrated' societies such as those of Melanesia — including, for example, Hagen. The stereotype says that what I can learn about a cluster of clans I can (more or less) replicate for the entire population, and talk of Hagen in the singular. This demographic simplicity is an illusion. But it seems to invite contrast with the situation in which I found myself writing about Elmdon in Essex, a village about the size of a Hagen clan. By no stretch of the imagination could I imagine it a microcosm of British society, or even white English society. That wider society is not graspable within the scope of the solitary fieldworker. It looks as though I can compare Hagen with this or that neighbor in the Papua New Guinea Highlands; I cannot even begin to compare the Essex village with the pit settlements of Durham or the suburbs of Manchester, in order to think about Britain in connection (say) with North America. More accurately, I cannot let the demographic scale somehow stand for theoretical intention.

In fact, places are not perceived as proper entities for comparison at all. Absurd to enumerate the similarities and differences between Elmdon as a rural community and the inhabitants of a Durham pit 'village' containing 10,000 people, or a crowded suburb of Manchester, a 'village' only in the name its residents give it. One can find connections — a common communication praxis or participation in the national economy (Fabian, pers. comm.), a 'loose coupling' (Schwimmer n.d. after Goffman). But there is no proportion between them, no encompassing scale or common context that will make these places units of a comparable order. Nor do they have the same internal structure; they are different kinds of entities. People's behavior and interactions are so differently contextualized that similar actions — how many times folk visit their relatives for instance — become incommensurable. I could almost say to myself that I experience myself as different persons in thinking about these different places.

But how is that experience constructed? What is this persuasive commonsense? The reason I feel those disjunctions is actually embedded within an imagery that I may well **share** with the residents of these places. The sense of dislocation — moving between different orders of complexity — is like moving between an intimate village and the outside world that pushes strangers in and sucks villagers out. The people of Elmdon think that way, and I gather it is not so different in the Durham mining villages, or in Manchester's Hulme which is part of one of the largest housing complexes in the country. I cannot compare the winding lanes of Elmdon with the high rise flats of Hulme, but I must also do more than simply juxtapose them in my mind. There is a connection between them if their inhabitants entertain apparently similar ideas. As well as the connections to be found, then, are the connections they voice, as in the common conceptualization of what a village is. They share their 'villages'. But those similar ideas disguise themselves by appearing as ideas **about** dissimilarity: they are ideas about how different everyone is from one another, how different different places are.[26]

In short, here we have the members of a plural society telling one another how plural everything is beyond 'the village'. Perhaps anthropologists' stereotyped defensiveness about the small-scale nature of their own forays into complex societies is part of the same phenomenon. Yet one need not be completely persuaded by the presentation of the village as a cosy/invaded community or kinship as a question of networks and family groups, or society as somehow a vast and complex entity that lies beyond the individual. Nor, in that case, must one necessarily think of persons as individuals circumscribed only by the complementarities of fixed centers or uncentered fragmentations.

To participate in this kind of homely thinking about persons and places is also to appreciate that no one realization of these ideas is equal to all the situations in which similar realizations are possible. They are used to different effect. To specify the circumstances under which realization and its effects are achieved requires a way of conceptualizing the partial nature of the connections, for instance, between the way the residents of Elmdon and of Hulme use these ideas. Tyler's aesthetic form — the journey — might work as an imaginative device through which to think about connections if we could dispense with its attendant presumption of integration taking place within a single entity.

Possibly it was because too much attention was given to getting rid of the 'one figure' of the fieldworker with her or his authoritative vision that Tyler rested his case on the therapeutic effect of listening to a composite of many voices. Yet that original figure of the fieldworker was only ever visible in certain places — anthropologists always claimed it would never do 'at home', and upturned it to expose its fragmented obverse. The image of the one person of the fieldworker with her/his perspectival vision, outside looking in, could not work. There is no immediate integration between her or his different perspectives if they can be experienced as the perspectives of different persons. Yet the obverse figure is not a simple composite of voices. This is a plurality: not a collage of experiences, but the person at once internally fragmented and externally a unit among a multiplicity of units. Or, to turn it another way, integration and fragmentation coalesce as personified forms of number.

The image of the person as an individual encourages us to regard number in a particular way — that we are dealing with ones (single entities), or else with a multiplicity of ones (innumerable entities). Two is already a plurality. This homely mathematics also compels us to see wholes made up of individual parts, center persons integrating a plurality of individuals as fragments of multiple centerings. Consequently, we seem caught between an atomistic view (a totality is constituted by the aggregation of independent elements) and a holistic one (where elements have no existence apart from a total structure or system) (Ingold 1986:43).

Villages and high rise flats are hardly commensurate units. People's habits and thoughts are not the customs of this or that community: the ideas of Elmdon people cannot be ascribed simply to the fact that they live in Elmdon. By the same token, we come to realize that there are connections between places. Yet the similarities between the residents of Elmdon, Durham, Hulme cannot rest on a comparison of the places themselves. These communities constitute neither a single phenomenon nor a multiplicity of phenomena.

P.2. Awkward Presences.   Comparative analysis in the traditional anthropological repertoire had one edge: it allowed the theorist to specify the difference between what was comparable and what was not, and offered the knowledge that one kind of activity is not necessarily equivalent to another but must be conceived in its context. In short, it worked with a strong sense of social and cultural contextualization. That in turn presented a concrete image of integration existing **outside the body** of the observer — one was describing a system that had internal connections or was comparing systems whose connections belonged to them and not just to the person perceiving them. It was a counterpart to the scholar's singular acts of synthesis. The power of such referential activity was to create a plurality of external referents, of 'societies' and 'cultures' as providing innumerable contexts for the subject of study.

Let me return briefly to the aesthetic integration proffered by ethnographic therapy. My earlier rendering neglected the point that experience is also imagined by these writers as taking place outside the (body of the) individual traveller/consumer. It may be the reader who must put things together out of a book such as Crapanzano's; but, of course, he or she does so at the invitation of the author. The connections he makes will prompt the reader's making or her or his own. Tyler's emergent mind of author-text-reader, with no individual locus but an infinity of loci, is just such an image of an 'outside' event — or rather of something that takes place neither within nor outside the person, for it can be attributed to the subjectivity of neither author nor reader.

To turn these ideas to anthropological use, one needs to turn the emergent mind with no individual locus into a much stronger sense of exteriority: to imagine a person as a 'someone' (Burridge 1979). One needs to restore a perception of other presences — of those who jostle, pressing in, as concrete and particular others who will neither go away nor merge with oneself. Between the event that takes place nowhere (it has no locus) and the individual subject of therapy, I wish to suggest a third way of personifying the ethnographic experience, to draw a figure who seems to be **more than** one person, indeed more than a person. What happens 'takes place' because it happens somewhere, in the presence of others, because events become interventions, the subjectivity of different persons the issue. However, these interruptions to the self do not guarantee a therapeutic return to the familiar. Rather, there is a sense of holding in one's grasp what cannot be held — of trying to make the body do more than it can do — of making a connection with others in a partial manner.

In that case, what form or figure or what kind of social relationship is being described? What image would contain within itself the idea of a person capable of making connections while knowing that they are not completely subsumed within her or his experience of them? That of itself can then be neither one nor a particle in a multiplicity of ones, neither sum nor fragment? I only ask the question because there is a model to hand for how one might sustain partial connections and an image of the kind of authorial 'person' that might in the circumstances carry aesthetic conviction. The model is of academic feminist discourse and the image of Donna Haraway's cyborg, half human, half machine.

P.2. POLITICS

P.1. FEMINIST CRITIQUE

P.1. VOICES

P.1. Interest Groups. "One story is not as good as another", states Haraway (1989:331). Attention to narrative, she continues, does not displace attention to science, but seeks to understand the story–laden forms of certain kinds of scientific practice — "as a condition of doing good science." Her subject here is primatology, but she intends the points more generally.

In an essay on the science question in feminism, she identifies activist feminist enquiry as belonging to a 'special interest group', along with any collective historical subject "that dares to resist the stripped down atomism of Star Wars, hyper-market, postmodern, media-simulated citizenship" (1988:575). She raises the familiar point that contesting an already constructed objectivity participates in the field of rhetoric that constructs it, with a twist. The problem, as she sees it, is how to have both an account of radical historical contingency for all claims to knowledge, **and** a (proportionate) commitment to truthful, faithful accounts of the world. Feminists might not need to master narratives, or to theorize about global systems, but they "do need an earth-wide network of connections, including the ability partially to translate knowledge among very different — and power-differentiated — communities" (1988:580). In these disassembled and disassembling times, how can one hold out a feminist version of objectivity?

The concept of an interest group implies a notion of perspective, and in a strong not weak sense. For what an interest group promotes is that very perspective itself: the 'point of view' from which the world is evaluated, and on whose behalf claims are made. Interests — the material objectives or grievances at issue, condition of life or whatever — determine the viewpoint of the campaigners. Competition is thus about what can be seen and how it is seen. A problem to which Haraway draws attention, however, is the contemporary sense that there is too much to see. In a world composed of multiple different perspectives, the very claim to a perspective is flattening. Now one could as equally use an aural metaphor — one can think of the clamor of tongues, of the voice standing for a debated position, and Haraway herself refers to rhetoric; I return to such a metaphor in a moment. But her interest in visualization is apposite, since she uses it to carry a specific argument about the perception of limits and possibilities, and the possibilities of a finite view.

Haraway comments on the visual greed of multinationalist postmodernist culture.[27]

> Vision in this technological feast becomes unregulated
> gluttony; all seems not just mythically about the godtrick
> of seeing everything from nowhere, but to have put the
> myth into ordinary practice (1988:581).

Yet the view of infinite vision is an illusion. It disembodies the seeing eye.

> [Rather, we] need to learn in our bodies, endowed with
> primate color and stereoscopic vision, how to attach the
> objective to our theoretical and political scanners in
> order to name where we are and are not, in dimensions
> of mental and physical space we hardly know how to name
> (1988:582).

Objectivity, then, she argues, turns out to be about particular and specific embodiments, not transcendence. Our pictures of the world depend on the active perceptual systems of bodily organs and prosthetic devices. They should not be allegories of infinite mobility and interchangeability but, as she puts it, "of elaborate specificity and difference and the loving care people might take to learn how to see faithfully from another's point of view" (1988:583). From this point of view, rational knowledge would not pretend to disengagement; partiality is the position of being heard and making claims, the view from a body rather than the view from above. All visual possibilities, therefore, are highly specific — only partial perspective, she declares, promises objective vision.

This is another ethnography for our times, then, simultaneously situating itself within the discourses to which it is party and retaining the participant's right to passionate criticism. Haraway's stance, vis-á-vis the culture of science to which she attends, is both to give it room and not to make it the only room she inhabits — the position of other people's viewpoints remains. But there is a further twist to her account, an unexpected dimension.

Learning to see faithfully from another's point of view, she writes, includes seeing faithfully "even when the other is our own machine" (1988:583). By machine she intends a double reference to embodiment: awareness of human bodies and their organs — including the highly specialized instrument of the eye — in terms of their 'mechanical' capacities and possibilities, and awareness of the machines through which one arrives at other 'perceptual' translations and ways of seeing. Bodies and machines are systems in themselves. And like bodies, we need to like machines enough to know their sensory capabilities: how from a camera on a space satellite one derives color photographs that can be assembled by the eye as planetary bodies — very detailed and very partial visions.

The evocation of space flight recalls the earlier metaphors of journey. The positioning of our journeys, the departures and returns we might imagine, is not simply to be imagined via the emergent mind that in Tyler's phrase has no locus. Our synthesizing organs are not only in the head. The body, so to speak, is always party to the imagining.

P.2. Partial Participants. Yet there is a domain of feminist activism that could be retrospectively imaginable as just such an emergent mind. One could almost say it flourishes from its sense of disembodiment. Its power is a certain dislocation.

Looking back over the recent history of feminist scholarship, it is possible to claim it as much for postmodernism as to see it as postmodernism's most trenchant critic. Though I do not pursue the point, there is, as Haraway adumbrates, prevalent internal resistance to the appropriation of feminism by the "mainstream 'corpus' of ideas and theories of postmodernism" (Lee 1987:9; cf. Hawkesworth 1989). Nonetheless, feminist scholarship appears as both precursor to and an enactment of some of the positions that we would now assemble under that latter name. Certainly, as they have impinged on anthropology, some forms of feminist scholarship have anticipated contemporary experimentation, and in many ways gone further. What is interesting is that feminist debate, as it takes place in scholarly journals and on the bookshelves, is a debate constructed as lying beyond the individual participants without necessarily being the object of a communal or corporate enterprise as a 'body' itself.

First, the debate makes an object, a focus for regard, out of a multiplicity of interests which have to be neither opposed nor reconciled. There is no agreed body of knowledge to which individuals must feel they are contributing. Feminist knowledge cannot be regarded in a cumulative sense as one might regard anthropological knowledge, producing material available for general scrutiny. Each item of academic feminist thinking, from history or psychology or literary criticism or biology or wherever, comes from a particular position. It meets on common ground — interest in promoting women's visibility — but scholars contribute their part by each being their own scholar. Those who do construct a focused 'feminist theory' divide themselves by political position — Radical, Socialist, Marxist, and so forth — though like the labels of contemporary political parties, the terms already seem old-fashioned. Internal relations are not regarded as homogeneous. Ann Game (1985:129) repeats a now well-established observation when she reviews the agreement "that it is not possible to speak about feminist theory: there are numerous feminist theories." It is not just a question of "simultaneous activity on multiple fronts" (Craig 1985:63), but of differences sustained between those fronts: "its multiple internal differences."

Second, then, feminist knowledge in particular disciplines really only works for those disciplines — that is, is kept attached to its (external) sources. The insights that one might bring to anthropology are not really of much interest to the historian of science or the literary critic: there is simply an analogy or parallelism between what we/they do. "They afford different ways of knowing" (DuBois *et al.* 1985:201). Sandra Harding is more emphatic: identifying two strands in feminist critiques of science, she argues that there are "good reasons to nourish the tendencies in each which conflict" (1986:654).

Third, then, in the nature of feminist enterprise, its academic practitioners are by definition never 'one person', 'just' a feminist. Or to put
it the other way round, a feminist is never a complete person.

The feminist position does not merely parallel the anthropologist's
belated postmodern stance; the endeavors are connected to one another.
They belong to coeval Western historical-cultural milieux, and if they have
been slow in making cross-references to each other (cf. M. Strathern 1986),
nonetheless may derive inspiration from similar sources.[28] The products
of academic feminist activity constitute discourse, not text, their polyphony
anticipating the anthropologists' rejection of "monophonic authority"
(Clifford 1986:15). One may draw a parallel between Tyler's insistence that
"there is no instance of a post-modern ethnography . . . Every attempt
will always be incomplete" (1986:136) and Judith Stacey's (1988) insistence
that we must be content with ethnographies that are ever only "partially
feminist." Indeed, Stacey extends Clifford's significant dictum about the
partial nature of ethnographic truths (cf. 1986:7) in a most interesting
manner. The paradox that faced her sociological study of family and gender
in California's Silicon Valley was how the ethnographer could overcome
an unfolding empathy between ethnographer and informant. The result
must be an ethnography that can only be partially feminist, for the
ethnographer is extended, drawn into mutualities that cannot be recovered
as ethnography and into writing an ethnography that cannot be recovered
as mutually feminist.

The idea of the partial nature of the ethnographic truths to be derived
from the anthropologist's fieldwork encounter was thus prefigured in the
way in which feminists spoke to one another from their different positions.
It is those differential positions that make them into partial persons: there
is a sense in which to be a feminist is necessarily to be someone else as
well. Feminism thus lies in 'the difference it makes' to other aspects of
one's identity. "Any feminist standpoint will necessarily be partial" (Flax
1987:642). As Stacey correspondingly implies, a person is only ever partially
feminist. This is not an issue of commitment or singlemindedness, but
of the networking of feminist discourse among quite other discourses.

Feminist scholarship has an edge, so to speak, in its cultural artefacts,
in its re-invention of the polyphony of social life within the confines of
its own concerns. The multi-, trans- or cross-disciplinary nature of its external
concerns signifies. Corresponding to no one viewpoint, 'it' cannot be
imagined as the (collective) voice of one person, and the position it provides
is the more striking for that. "**Despite** the diversity of its arguments, feminism
is unified through its challenge to male power" (Currie and Kazi 1987:77,
my emphasis). Conversely, it palpably exists beyond the comprehension
or grasp of any individual scholar: pluralism creates a discourse encompassable by no single participant. This is not because its range is too vast

or complex to be grasped, but because of the way these external differences connect to internal ones.

For, importantly, this debate between and across different disciplines is not definable by those disciplines either. As external reference points, they are themselves mediated and eclipsed by the internal political imagery, by what 'kind' of feminism is at issue. These internal differences intervene as a source of counter differentiation insofar as they are constructed in relation to one another (Eisenstein 1984:xix).[29] The internal positions are not mere juxtapositions; they do not amount, *pace* Harding (1986:657), to an "articulation of relativism." And they do not compose pastiche, "blank parody that has lost its sense of humour" (Jameson 1985:114), "irony which has foregone its critical dimension" (Webster 1987:58). On the contrary, Haraway makes the concept of irony yield a different image. "Irony is about contradictions that do not resolve into larger wholes, even dialectically, **about the tension of holding incompatible things together** because both or all are necessary and true" (1985:65, my emphasis). Things hold together: we contemplate not a succession of styles which work only to echo one another, but a working compatibility.

Feminist debate is characterized by a compatibility that does not require comparability between the persons who engage in it, bar their engaging in it. Whether in terms of internal **or** external differences, persons travel between different positions. It is almost as though the disproportion were deliberate. Feminist scholarship is not a discipline isomorphic with other disciplines — it simply invades and draws on them. Thus I cannot substitute feminism for anthropology or vice versa, listen to one and forget the other (cf. Moore 1988). At the same time, each constitutes a position from which to regard a counter position.

Now this disjunction or partition between feminism and anthropology is not the kind of partition suggested by the metaphor of locality. There is no walking away from one 'place' into another. Neither discipline offers a room of its own in whose refuge I can be constituted as a whole person; neither is a complete context, and when they are thought of as contexts for my actions, I am equal to neither. At the same time, they do not constitute halves of a whole: I do not have a feminist side and an anthropological side, no alternating facades. Nor will the metaphor of debate or conversation do completely. One does not simply take turns with oneself, managing an endless internal dialogue as though one were a collectivity of participants. Finally, it is not simply a question of two perspectives. For the entity who experiences is neither two different persons nor one person divided into two.

From this subjective point of view, awareness of different voices is both more and less than the imagery of a disembodiment — separate rooms, separate conversations — suggests. But if each 'side' affords a position from which to see the other, perhaps we might use the analogy of embodiment itself. When each becomes the ground and medium from which and through which to perceive the other, the attendant awareness is imaginable as the consciousness of a person knowing s/he is seeing from and through the body s/he inhabits.

P.2. BODIES

P.1. One is Too Few but Two are Too Many. Haraway's analogy between bodies and machines was intended to draw attention to the mechanical or physiological specificity of all visualizations of the world. But her analogy echoes an earlier paper (1985) whose central image has now made it something of a classic. The image is of a cyborg, an entity that is neither body nor machine.

A cyborg is neither body nor machine in that the principles upon which its different parts work form no single system. Its parts are neither proportionate to nor disproportionate from one another. Its internal connections comprise an integrated circuit, but not a single unit. This is how Haraway's image also works: it is a whole image but not an image of a whole. For it brings together the imaginary and the real. The image is both of a hypothetical entity, a cyborg connected to others in an imaginary world of cyborgs, and of its context or reference points, that is, the connection of circumstances in the world today that make it useful to think with.

Cyborgs are a cybernetic fantasy dreamed up by science fiction, creatures partly animate, partly technologized — human beings implanted with devices or machines incorporating human organs, the hybrids of transplant and genetic manipulation. At the same time, the fiction is realized in an already existing post-scientific world where

> [m]icroelectronics mediate the translations of labor into robotics and word processing; sex into genetic engineering and reproductive technologies; and mind into artificial intelligence and decision procedures (1985:84, emphasis removed).

It no longer becomes possible to sustain a division between the natural and the artificial, between matter and consciousness, or between who makes and who is made in the relations between human and machine. "It is not clear what is mind and what body in machines that resolve into coding practices" (1985:97). Biological organisms have ceased to exist as objects of knowledge; their place is taken by biotic components. "There is," Haraway (1985:97) argues, "no fundamental, ontological separation in our formal knowledge of machine and organism, of technical and organic." The loss of distinction between mind and body or nature and culture is mirrored by the merging of organism and machine itself: the vision of machines as "prosthetic devices, intimate components, friendly selves" (1985:97). With such allies there is no need to yearn after organic unity.

What moves Haraway's critique are the unities by which people — including feminists — have tried to overcome the idea of a dichotomous or divided world with the idea that societies might be communities or that labor might be unalienated. Such visions of totality inevitably perpetuate the grounding dualisms which they seek to collapse. Cyborgs set different thoughts in train.

Cyborgs may be needy for connection, she puts it, but are wary of organicism. "Organicism," writes Haraway (1986:86), "is the analytical longing for a natural body, for purity outside the disruptions of the 'artificial'. It is the reversed, mirror image of other forms of longing for transcendence . . . Feminism must be opposed to holistic organicisms, if it is to avoid [the] logics and practises of organic domination . . . My hope is that cyborgs relate difference by partial connection rather than antagonistic opposition, functional regulation, or mystic function." A cyborg "does not seek unitary identity and so generate antagonistic dualisms without end" (1985:99); it has no single boundary, and its parts do not comprise internal divisions; it will not dream of the original family or of the Garden of Eden. "The cyborg is a creature in a post-gender world; it has no truck with bisexuality, pre-Oedipal symbiosis, unalienated labor, or other seductions to organic wholeness through a final appropriation of all the powers of the parts into a higher unity" (1985:67). The relationships for forming totalities from parts are questioned, as are the relationships of domination and hierarchy promoted by the dualities of encompassment — such as self and other, public and private, or body and mind.[30] Above all, "nature and culture are reworked: the one can no longer be the resource for appropriation or incorporation by the other" (1985:67). That earlier perception belonged to a world structured by divisions and dichotomies, where, in struggling to be free of machines, people perceived themselves to be dominated by them.

She adds, "The machine is not an it to be animated, worshipped and dominated. The machine is us, our processes, an aspect of our embodiment" (1985:99, original emphasis). Machines do not replicate human experience and Haraway is not saying that organisms are modelled on machines. On the contrary, the point is to see a difference. The question is the kind of connection one might conceive between entities that are made and reproduced in different ways — have different origins in that sense — but which work together. Mind, body and tool, she writes *apropos* communications sciences, can be on very intimate terms.

Perhaps one can re-introduce image into this intimate set. I argued earlier that there is no possibility of restoring the plausibility that outmoded images have lost. In her 1985 paper, Haraway underlines the argument that in this sense postmodernism is not an option, a style among others, any more than modernism once was: it is not something which one might actually be for or against. Rather, we live in a context where we have been made to see things differently. Nothing can substitute for loss of conviction but a new conviction. And the present conviction is that "there is no longer any place from without that gives meaning to the comforting fiction of critical distance" (1985:69). She states:

> My position is that feminists (and others) need continu-
> ous cultural reinvention, postmodernist critique, and
> historical materialism; only a cyborg would have a chance.

Haraway's account is moved by the limitation of imagining that one can resolve difference through appeal to organic unity because she wishes to delimit a politics beyond the sinister entailment of single visions:

> a cyborg world might be about lived social and bodily
> realities in which people are not afraid of . . . permanently
> partial identities and contradictory standpoints. The
> political struggle is to see from both ['animal' and
> 'machine'] perspectives at once because each reveals
> . . . dominations and possibilities unimaginable from the
> other vantage point (1985:72).

I have my own interest in Haraway's political cyborg. It carries a certain aesthetic conviction, persuades by its form. If the motive for her writings is to create networks of communication between people who do not require to be bound by appeal to common unity or origin, but who are connected as different, exterior presences to one another, she offers an imaginative entry into how we might conceive the conduct of social relationships.

P.2. A Hidden Extension.   The cyborg supposes what it could be like to make connections without assumptions of comparability. Thus might one suppose a relation between anthropology and feminism: were each a realization or extension of the capacity of the other, the relation would be of neither equality nor encompassment. It would be prosthetic, as between a person and a tool.[31] Compatibility without comparability: each extends the other, but only from the other's position. What the extensions yield are different capacities. In this view, there is no subject-object relation between a person and a tool, only an expanded or realized capability.
   My intimation of person-tool reciprocity momentarily invites the absurd. Yet one often has the counter-thought, that the human body has no mind

of its own! In truth, an organic heart inhabits a body that also has a mind, whereas a mechanical heart is a simulation not attached to any mind of its own, and to appear to impute subjectivity or intention to the latter seems ludicrous. Of course I do not. These are anthropomorphic tropes an anthropomorph must create in order to see things from the machine's point of view — that is, grasp the specificity of the perceptual processes by which we see via machines.

Translated into academic terms, this view provides a way of thinking about access to different worlds, different audiences. Thus, when 'I' think of myself as an anthropologist, feminist scholarship becomes an aid or tool; it introduces thoughts I would not otherwise entertain. Hence an anthropologist can make feminist discourse exist as a distinct exterior presence — 'outside' the body, as it were, because it is an extension of it, an instrument made of different materials, and able to do things that the original body alone cannot. At the same time, a tool only works for as long as it remains attached — it is an instrument for one person's interactions with others, but not something to be encompassed or possessed independently of that person's use of it.

Does this extend our way of thinking about the partial connections of a conversation? I return to my example. Feminist discourse creates connections between the participants — but they remain partial insofar as they create no single entity between them. What each creates is an extension of a position, which could not be done without the instrument of the conversation but in the end is done from the position each occupies for herself or himself. 'Partial' captures the nature of the interlocution well, for not only is there no totality, each part also defines a partisan position. Ethnographic truths are similarly partial in being at once incomplete and committed (Clifford 1986:7).

I am using the connected, non-comparable parts of a cyborg in a double way. First, the notion of a machine connected to an organism in the way a tool extends the body suggests a connection between entities based on the fact that each realizes capacities for the other: each makes the other 'work'. Thus may one imagine the relationship between a person and his or her thoughts, or of one's thoughts and how one converses with others, or of scholars from different backgrounds engaging in a feminist conversation. In none of these cases is the realization or extension equal to what it is attached to or where it originates from. Haraway talks of cyborgs as capable of regeneration but not reproduction. The one component is of different order from the other, and is not created by what creates that other. They are not built to one another's scale. As Haraway also says, in the same way the politics of a postscientific world must talk not of rebirth, producing something equal to its producer, but of regeneration, that is, extension. I can make a conversation work for me as a tool works, as I can make myself work in sustaining the conversation.

Second, the lack of proportion is not to be reimagined in terms of parts and total systems. At first sight, a 'tool' still suggests a possible encompassment by the maker and user who determines its use. Yet our theories of culture already tell us that we perceive uses **through** the tools we have at our disposal. Organism and machine are not connected in a part/totality relationship, if the one cannot completely define the other. Switching perspectives — as between anthropology and feminism — requires neither that a position left behind is obliterated nor that it is subsumed.[32] In turn, neither position offers an encompassing context or inclusive perspective. Rather, each exists as a localized, embodied vision. To be an anthropologist is to use feminist scholarship as a resource for or as an extension of anthropological insights, just as to be an organism rather than a machine is to extend organic possibilities.

Here one position could almost be thought of as constituted by another in the way that social relations are imagined in certain anthropological discourses as constitutive of persons. The presence of specific exterior others that provides a place for the individual person elicits from him or her a perception of those social relationships as connections at once part and not part of her or himself. Perhaps such a sense of positioning may also be created not just by the specificity of the presences (persons who are each 'someone') but by a history that does not otherwise need to be present. All that needs to be known is that these others have come from 'somewhere', that they have a perspective that does not quite constitute a perspective for oneself.

P.2.   INTRUSIONS AND COMPARISONS

P.1. INTRUSIONS

P.1. Techniques of Control. I have not adequately conveyed the frightening techno-military background against which Haraway creates her scaled-down cyborg of almost human dimensions, the totalizing world visions against which she seeks to evoke a web of muted but audible communications. On the face of it, in my account, the cyborg image therefore seems just too friendly.[35] How can we tell the difference between an extension or realization of human capacity and its perversion or subversion? Should we not introduce a difference between the tool that extends the capability of the user and the machine that incorporates the operator into its determining system (Ingold 1988)? When persons are controlled through the routine of machines, being tied to the rhythm of an engine is a diminishing, not an enhancing, exercise. Tools under the control of others may be seen simply as machines in this sense, as I would read the point recently reiterated in the **Feminist Review.**

> [Where] tools necessary for producing objects are owned privately . . . [l] abourers are no longer free to produce objects that express their own ideas or needs. Instead, they must sell their labour-power to a capitalist and so become an abstract 'extension' of the tool. Through their labour, producers no longer give material expression to their own ideas but to the ideas of others who design products that will bring a return on the capital invested (Currie and Kazi 1987:85).

What appears 'extended' in this instance is the power of those who control the entire process; they turn tools for themselves into machines for others as instruments of their domination.

Aihwa Ong (1987a) points to the case of Third World women engaged in high-tech industrial processes, where innovative technology leads to new forms of oppression. In fact she observes that, in electronics manufacturing, women's very gender has been disassembled through their literal attachment to machines. Her example is from factory regimes in Malaysia (and see 1987b). On the one hand, the extreme decomposition of the tasks requires workers to do repetitive and minute jobs; on the other hand, management seeks to control women's self-perception by talking about their natural ability to withstand the work (1987a:622). But there is more than this: depending on their own cultural origins, the industrial corporations either define women workers as girls needing managerial protection (Japanese) or define them as consumers whose interest for others lies in their sexual identity (American). As a result

> [f]or women brought together in high-tech industry, gender has been disassembled. Microchip production has been defined as intrinsically 'feminine', women's fingers and eyes coded as extensions of electronic instrumentality and women's capabilities and subjectivities reduced to pure sexuality, . . . their relations with technology, men, and institutions . . . eroticized (1988:623-624).

The machines and bodies in question are indeed extensions, but constitute extensions of persons other than those who appear immediately tied to them. If this is another version of the cyborg, it only seems benign when it is abstracted from the nexus of power relationships where human capabilities are ordinarily exercised, as though all one had to think about were the immediate subject and his or her prosthesis.

But the unpleasantness of an image does not in itself guarantee social truth. The above paragraph could equally be applied to the figure of the tourist. Inevitably, this figure is doomed to appear in anthropological accounts in a luckless light. I take 'the tourist' as the person who seeks to extend personal experiences through the sampling or consuming of other cultures in a way that enhances a sense of her or his own. In this view, s/he is simply a consumer, a cultural glutton, engorged with the world's diversity. The bloated imagery is certainly unpleasant. In another view, however, the tourist may seem instead an unwitting extension of the host society, of other persons.

Thinking about certain of the social encounters in which tourists engage, Frederick Errington and Deborah Gewertz (1989) identify the need to attend to politics. Malcolm Crick's (1985) playful comparison between anthropology and tourism is not sufficient. They criticize the totalizing vision of the world for which he seems to write — the prevalent "postmodern perception that social life (including the disciplines that examine social life), in its fragmentation and multiplicity, is not an order" (1989:38, emphasis removed). Negotiation or play with form may seem to characterize the kinds of interactions in which people engage, but, they state, "in a world in which it profoundly matters who controls the terms of the interactions — the negotiations — and who wins or loses, anthropology needs not a heightened sense of the ludic but of the political" (1989:39).

Errington and Gewertz describe the accommodation of tourists, and of self-styled 'travellers', by people who live along the Sepik River in Papua New Guinea. Specifically, the authors take up a position from Chambri, regularly visited by tourists who have now come to play a major role in Chambri life itself.[34] During a field trip in 1987, they witnessed a 'ritual' put on for the double benefit of a set of initiates, who were teased and hazed, and of a party of tourists, who were openly invited to photograph the events. The organizer of the ritual was counting on admission fees from the latter to contribute to the very substantial outlay he had to make in order to see that the initiation of the former was satisfactorily executed. He was thus hoping to attract several groups of tourists during the month-long sequence of events. On this occasion, proceedings were delayed to coincide with the arrival of the appropriate boatload.

But events did not turn out quite as benignly as this description so far suggests. After the session, both tourists and initiates apparently emerged from the men's house confused, irritated and anxious. The initiates complained they had been handled too roughly; the tourists found the performance too violent, their own role too openly advertised (not only were initiates lined up, dusty and bleeding, to have their pictures taken, but the tourists were ordered — in English — to clap). They had been caught up in the machinery.

In their analysis, Errington and Gewertz comment that the presence of the outsiders in fact diminished the ferocity of the hazers' behavior towards the initiates. But what took its place was a kind of ridicule. If the initiates felt impotent, so did the tourists: they were witnessing something they could have described as authentic if it were not for very deliberate inclusion of themselves in the proceedings. They were required to assent to a performance in which in the final act they too became victims — the rubbish and ridicule poured on the heads of the initiates was somehow turned on them as well. In short, they were "partial targets" (1989:50-51). Perhaps in the same way as the initiates' bodies were being used as extensions of the hazers' control over their own cultural forms, so too the awkward and sweat-streaked presence of the tourists, like so many external bodies of the hazers, served to demonstrate the power of bodily control itself.

P.2. Cross-cultural Impasse. There is a further dimension to Errington and Gewertz's account. Their intention is to find a place for the anthropologist that is not preempted by the tourist, nor by the traveller as opposed to the tourist, nor for that matter by Chambri as opposed to everyone. Their objection is that the very susceptibility to the totalizing allurements of postmodern discourse makes anthropologists into tourists, and that there are other options. One at least involves retaining a sense of the power relations involved in encounters such as these. They make it clear (see Errington and Gewertz 1987) that the solution does not necessarily rest in the presentation of dialogue or even the presentation of 'other voices': the anthropologist may have to accede to the partisanship of others, including, whether they like it or not, reproducing other people's monologues, and thus other people's particular political interests.

I have evoked an image of real-life cyborg operatives caught up in the machination of other interests, of the tourist who is only half aware of what s/he is being subjected to, in order to make a rather obvious point about social life. There is nothing inherently benign about entering into relationships, or making everyone a participant in one's performance. We cannot use sociality as some kind of field that simply enhances personal or cultural awareness. Our academic cosmopolitans cannot just 'add on' social relationships to their experience of the world. On the contrary, against the present flow of cultural studies, one hears the voices of those who would restore the perspective of society, world system, and so forth, and with it fresh questions about the social relations of domination and power and the social objects people make out of their interactions.

Fabian (1983), among others, has argued that an anthropologist's own awareness of the objects created by their study cannot 'work' in his or her accounts until the subjects of the study are also seen to exist as coeval presences. At least, accounts must be co-temporalized, in order to make both past and present apparent. "The need to go there (to exotic places, be they far away or around the corner) is really our desire to be here (to find our position in the world)" (Fabian n.d.:3, emphasis removed). Both movements, he adds, converge on 'presence'. This is a statement not simply about cultural representation but about social relationships.

The study of culture certainly does not exhaust the task of anthropology. Indeed, Fabian (1985) registers an open complaint against its appropriation of anthropology. In the decades that preceded the present reflexive turn, and have thus to a large extent molded its form, culture gained its currency "as a cover-all concept and its historical function as a *point de repère* in our discipline by serving as a short term for a theory of knowledge" (1985:7). Anthropology, of course, he observes, has no monopoly on the concept of culture, a point Clifford also makes for the concept of ethnography. "A modern 'ethnography' of conjunctures, constantly moving between cultures, does not, like its Western alter ego 'anthropology', aspire to survey the full range of human diversity or development" (Clifford 1989:9, emphasis removed); rather, it perpetually displaces itself with the twentieth century's "unprecedented overlay of traditions." Nonetheless, the persistent anthropological equation of culture with tradition concerns Fabian. He argues (1985) that the very concept of culture is a nostalgic gesture towards disappearing forms of life, optimistically used to explain away as cultural 'variation' what in many cases has been the result of social discrimination and violence.

The emergence of culture as the focus for anthropological enquiry led to representationism as a key point of debate. It is not surprising, therefore, that the present critiques of representation turn on some other mode of conveying cultural experience. We have to revise our allegiance, Fabian suggests, not just to representationism but to the concept of culture itself.

Friedman (1987) mounted a similar attack about the same time.[35] Culture, he observes, has become a rallying point for several disciplines, the key term on which academics seem to be able to join debate, and has triumphed in anthropology, slipping into its postmodern form where all difference is cultural difference. The history of anthropology itself becomes understood not as a sequence of models or paradigms but of genres (1987:168). Yet, Friedman argues, if all possible statements are cultural statements, there is no epistemological distinction to be made between theoretical and cultural ones — a point, of course, with which the targets for his attack might well agree. But what he wishes to put in its place is a social theory that will understand its own process of production, including such gestures towards relativism. Difference and the perception of difference is a historical product, he argues, and anthropology must therefore be concerned both with the construction of its objects and with the social systems and material conditions that produce them. Both are the outcome of relations.

> 'Culture' is a particular way of objectifying the world in our kind of civilization — one that cannot be reduced to a universal notion of otherness. The latter must be understood in terms of the specificity of 'our' relation to 'them' over time, a conceptual configuration embedded in a material process (Friedman 1987:165).

I do not wish to rehearse all the arguments about the social production of knowledge, nor indeed their obverse, the cultural coding of power relations. Rather, there is a curious comment to be made about these academic dialogues themselves. For I suspect one could make either the epithet 'cultural' or the epithet 'social' do one's discriminating work. One could be as radical or critical from the point of view of culture or genre as from the point of view of society or social formation.

We are back to the question of scale: for the cultural critique of global systems can be quite as undermining as the social critique of the privileging of culture as a theory of knowledge. We strive to be situated — Haraway's embedded and embodied knowledges — but each situation carries its own burden of specificity. Just adding a bit of 'history' certainly will not do, even where by history we mean to recall power relations, specific forms of domination and relations of production. Each fresh dimension — a grasp of 'historical' location, of 'material' conditions, of 'social' relations — works momentarily to restore a sense of the concrete, to provide an illuminating context, and then becomes diffused within the convolutions of its own details. So we find that a sense of 'culture' or 'rhetoric' or 'narrative' will after all restore some of the now dissipated concreteness. 'Social' and 'cultural' dimensions behave like different scales of the anthropological enterprise. Either constellation would seem to give us access to what is here taken as real, viz. relations of power.

Scales become apparent through scale shift. One such shift is eloquently adumbrated by Kirsten Hastrup (n.d.) It turns on Fabian's plea for coevalness, but solves the issue of making the presence of others known by suggesting that far from 'historicizing' our accounts we should reinstate the tense of the ethnographic present. She argues that the literary concerns of postmodern anthropology displace realism as a genre but not realism as epistemology. Anthropology continues to posit 'real' differences. At the same time, the writing of ethnography composes a knowledge of a specific kind, one that transcends the empirical, as she puts it. Ethnographic knowledge is necessarily 'out of time.'

Hastrup provocatively suggests that "the ethnographic present must be redeemed as the discursive instance of anthropology" (n.d.:29). The problem with a historicizing approach is its claims to have exhausted a temporal moment, though one may remark this was never Fabian's intention (on the contrary he states that is "in order to be knowingly in each other's present" that we should share each other's pasts (1983:92)). Her specific point is that fieldwork experience is memory before it becomes text, and the author's engagement is always with his or her present memories — the past is not past. "The dialogue was 'then', but the discourse is 'now'. There is no choice of tense" (n.d.:28). Nothing else can render the truth about the absent reality. Ethnography, she suggests, can be seen as neither modern nor postmodern: it was always 'non-modern', and always hierarchical. Acknowledgment of its hierarchical nature, its partisanship, of authorial possessiveness, is what is required: "at the level of discourse, the 'others' are textually fixed; the absent people are recognized as embodying an alternative culture" (n.d.:31).

This argument returns us to the question of how to deal with what we perceive as (internal) differences **between** all those others. The question is exactly how to formulate the kinds of relations and connections at issue in the cross-societal comparisons once central to the anthropological job description. Comparative analysis might be more than a nostalgic reminder of past certainties. But what are we to choose as the scale? And it is for an aspect of that question that the idea of the cyborg could be useful. Stripped of friendly and unfriendly connotations alike, it might offer a way of imagining connections on their own scale(s).

P.2. COMPARISONS

P.1. Units for Comparative Analysis. Also in 1987, the **Annual Review of Anthropology** published an article on cross-cultural surveys. Its concern is recent refinements in statistical sensitivity to complex data, and notes for instance the revolutionary proliferation of methods for multivariate analysis (Burton and White 1987:148). The problem of comparing like units is disposed by reference to Murdock's early solution. Societies — Tikopia and China are their examples — may be at 'different levels of complexity or scale', but sampling from 'cultural provinces' or 'particular communities' apparently overcomes this.[36] The authors dwell at length on Galton's problem, however, one that also preoccupied an earlier review (J. Jorgensen 1979). The brief history of this classic problem is worth repeating.

It concerns a paper that Edward Tylor read to the [Royal] Anthropological Institute in 1888, which attempted to explain the development of a cluster of institutions to do with marriage and kinship by organizing data from a worldwide sample of 350 societies. Francis Galton, the then President, heard Tylor give his paper, and asked him about the independence of each unit: "the degree in which the customs of the tribes and races which are compared together are independent, instead of duplicate copies of the same original" (quoted in Stocking 1987:318). As Joseph Jorgensen succinctly puts it, Tylor could not answer Galton's question.

> Tylor had not produced maps locating each society in his sample or locating the distribution of each variable . . .The mapping of variables would have allowed Tylor to determine the propinquity at least of similar practices and hence provide a means to assess the likelihood, say, that the descent customs of some societies influenced the descent customs of other societies . . . [H]e failed to distinguish which of the institutional similarities possessed by groups of tribes in his sample had been inherited from a protoculture (two or more societies speaking sister languages and sharing cultural features that they inherited from a mother society from which they splintered), or had been acquired through borrowing, and which of the institutional similarities among tribes had been independently invented (J. Jorgensen 1979:313).

The author himself is one of those scholars who, on Burton and White's account, has made the issue of 'intersocietal connections' a part of his research programme.

I have no familiarity with the statistical modelling of these problems, but for discursive interest reproduce the terms in which Michael Burton and Douglas White argue (1987:146-7, my emphasis, references omitted).

> Galton's problem pertains to the non-independence of sampling units . . . The problem is not unique to cross-cultural comparisons but occurs in any study where there are **linkages** of kinship, interaction, or common heritage

among units of study, including biological heritage . . .
The problem goes beyond mere regional clustering of
traits. Regional clustering per se can be the result of
independent adaptations of societies to geographically
clustered environmental features. Only if the values of
a trait for a group of societies are significantly different
from those predicted by functional adaptations, and if
these deviations can be explained by the position of
societies in a regionally or historically based network,
do we have an instance of Galton's problem . . .
The network autocorrelation solution to Galton's problem . . . explicitly measures the effects of **linkages between
societies** upon their traits. This procedure has the ad-
vantage of bringing history, and the world system, back
into cross-cultural analysis, rather than trying to make
these important phenomena disappear from the sample.
The first stage of a network autocorrelation analysis is
**to compute the network of observed relationships among
societies** . . . Historical relatedness . . . is usually measured
by relationships among languages. This is a defensible
approach, since . . . language similarity provides a good
index of shared culture history, including migration from
a common origin.

Statistical analysis provides, in a sense, its own scale. The correlations
in question are, it would seem, correlations between entities modelled on
the image of 'linkages between societies.' Societies are not necessarily being
taken as independent and discrete units — the whole point of the sophisticated
correlation techniques is to show their interdependence — but their attributes
can be plotted by the position they occupy on common scales. Different
'levels' of phenomena provide different ranges of points. Societies,
communities, regions thus form one such scale, while a range of behavioral
traits such as harsh and affectionate socialization or of social institutions
such as patriliny and warfare presumably form others. At any one level
(scale), enumeration seems possible. Thus if "[b]ridewealth and patrilineal
inheritance are predicted by polygyny" (1987:153), these constitute a
comparable order of phenomena whose relative occurrence can be
enumerated. I have no debate with the methods. What is of interest is
the language that the practitioners, at certain points, seem to share in
common with others in their approach to cross-cultural comparison.

To take one example, Burton and White (1987:152) quote a study by
Paige and Paige (1981) [I have not consulted it independently] whose

primary hypothesis is that 'ritual is a form of political

bargaining that takes place in the absence of more formal mechanisms for asserting claims and adjudicating disputes. . .' [1981:69]. In this analysis, reproductive rituals such as menarchal rites, male circumcision, couvade and menstrual restrictions are varying ways men assert claims over women and children. Variation in the form of control by men is dependent upon the quality of the society's resource base and the size of the fraternal interest groups.

Although they go on to say that authors of the study find strong relationships between their two independent variables and four kinds of reproductive rituals, it is clear that the comparative intention could have been phrased in either statistical or discursive language. The examples touch on just the kinds of factors that Melanesianists, for instance, discuss. Now I infer that while it is socio-cultural attributes (such as presence or absence of male circumcision) that are being compared, incidence is implied by virtue of the location of these elements 'in' this or that society/culture or community (cf. J. Jorgensen 1979:311-12). Different variables will, of course, differentially locate the social unit from which they come. But while there is no final sum, crudely put, the outcome must be that societies and cultures are at some moment being counted too. However overlap is computed, the question is 'where' the attributes are found. This is also a habit of some discursive practice. It is not necessary to be interested in probablistic or correlational computation in order to think of societies and/or customs in terms of the numerical occurrence of instances.

P.2. Partial Connections. Various positions jumped or traversed earlier have indicated some of the questions that lie in the path of discursive approaches to comparison. Reflections on the form of narration and the otherness of one's subject matter are also reflections on the kinds of connections these concepts make possible.[37] Correlations are not social relations, but perhaps social relations do indeed provide a model of sorts for the connecting of phenomena. Hence the humanoid figure who has run through the account adopts a posture, a kind of presence, that both is and is not the anthropologist.

To draw a comparison, or make an analogy, is not necessarily to impute connection: it may indicate a resemblance, rather than a relation, and the resemblance may be fantastic, rather than real, 'magical' (Jackson 1987). Yet the very act of comparing also constitutes a making of connections, and evokes a metaphorical relationship. Michael Jackson (1987:21) notes: "[T]he fact that things are used on the basis of magical similitudes does not preclude their having intellectual and therapeutic value." Conversely, using the similitudes gives things a value: comparison — intellectual, therapeutic — creates their multiplicity.

The detour into the everyday world of the English and accompanying Western preoccupations with feminism and postmodernism seemed to underline a problem that people in complex societies have: they have complex problems. The traditional image of the single fieldworker did at least suggest counter relief, that simpler societies have simpler problems. But, of course, there is no relief. On the contrary, anthropologists have created considerable difficulties for themselves in their numerical vision of a world full of societies and cultures. The problem as it is perceived is both how to connect them and what to do with the connections between them.

Holy (1987) documents a past shift in assumptions about comparative procedures. These moved from establishing 'positivistic' functional correlations which aimed for generalizations across cultures to using comparison to facilitate 'interpretative' descriptions, which aimed for the adequate analytical translation of individual systems. Both procedures have had their critics, and questions have been constantly asked about comparability. On the one hand, the now familiar doubts about definitional boundaries and the units of analysis have plagued the pursuit of functional correlations; on the other hand have lain all the anxieties of translation, and the impossibility of rendering one world view in terms of another (e.g. Overing 1987). The first set of problems arose from attempts to generalize across disparate cultural situations; the second from juxtaposing alien systems to those of the West. But there is a further problem, given by circumstances which — as the contributors to Holy's volume attest — on the surface look most amenable to discursive if not statistical application: the comparison of societies and socio-cultural elements within a specific region.[38] However, discursive no less than statistical analysis has run into difficulties with number.

The Papua New Guinea Highlands provides an example of the problem, interesting since it was opened to study at a period in anthropological history when comparative analysis was taken for granted as the definitive feature of the subject. Here we have information on several social systems, with demonstrated gradients between styles of leadership, horticultural practices, group formation, exchange relationships, the nature of cult and ceremonial life, and so on. There is no dearth of rounded studies, monographs full of insight into ritual detail or economic relations, countless evocations of world views. The circumstances appear perfect for internal comparison. Yet most ethnographers have usually made forays into adjacent societies and cultures in order better to specify the particularity of their own ethnographic findings or else compared two or three clusters, like regions within regions. We are left with the troubling multiplicity of instances.

This in turn comes from the particular way that anthropologists by and large have been encouraged to think of number, that the alternative to one is many. Consequently we either deal with ones, namely single societies or attributes, or else with a multiplicity of ones brought together for some purpose. Relationships must somehow exist outside or between these phenomena, for it is gathering the phenomena together that makes the connections. The very notion of a correlation is almost of an entity hanging somewhat like an emergent mind that could occupy, if they existed, spaces between societies.[39] To plot societies against this or that variable creates the image of an interstellar void traversed by the imaginary lines of a 'relationship'.

A world obsessed with ones and the multiplications and divisions of ones creates problems for the conceptualization of relationships. To be able to conceive of persons as more than atomistic individuals but less that subscribers to a holistic community of shared meanings would be of immediate interest for comparative analysis. Anthropologists already know all the pitfalls associated with representing societies and cultures as though they themselves were unique, bounded individuals. The question is how to think about the connections between them in a way that does not have to rest on that premise.

$$*\quad*\quad*\quad*\quad*\quad*$$

If the impasse does indeed lie in the simplicity of the arithmetic, there are diverse theoretical turns one could take. It is possible to conceive of similarities and differences between societies through coefficients or scalogram matrices (J. Jorgensen 1979) that measure propinquity; or to turn to poststructuralist discourse, and find 'difference' itself conceptualized as a journey — "Differences always take us **elsewhere**, we might say, involve us in an ever proliferating network of displacement and deferral of meaning" (Moi 1985:153, original emphasis). It is also possible simply to cut short the whole discussion with an observation such as that of Leo Howe: he slices through various confusions surrounding the issue of comparison by succinctly noting that it is not a matter of looking for things that are similar or different in themselves and then comparing them, but realizing that, by virtue of its selectivity, the comparative process itself creates relations of similarity and difference (1987:136). Comparability is not intrinsic to anything.[40]

The point of comparison is, he suggests, to illuminate one set of ill-understood phenomena by reference to another set more clearly comprehended. The choice of what phenomena to compare will be determined by many factors, including the researcher's theoretical purposes. We could, then, rest with the figure of the researcher who knows to what purpose he or she is creating similarity and difference in the data to hand. Howe makes the point beautifully, and the rest would be a relief. Yet to conceive of degrees of understanding is **already** to introduce a disproportion within the researcher's mind. The researcher must connect better and less well-conceived thoughts. If there is any value in carrying the discussion forward, it is because the question of proportionate description remains in the anthropological account.

I dwelt on the cyborg insofar as that humanoid figure confronts the sense of proportion. The cyborg observes no scale: it is neither singular nor plural, neither one nor many, a circuit of connections that joins parts that cannot be compared insofar as they are not insomorphic with one another. It cannot be approached holistically or atomistically, as an entity or as a multiplication of entities. It replicates an interesting complexity.

The societies of the Papua New Guinea Highlands, and elements of their formation, are complex parts and uneven outgrowths of one another. If they are connected, they are only partially so. The continuities I have in mind are less a question of abstract similarities (Parkin 1987) than of proximities in space and time (Fardon 1987). From the contemporary location of any one Highlands society, particular others will look like variants of itself, and thus each will appear as a **variant of some other concrete form**. These societies exist in the first place as a result of people's communications, and in their communications people are always expanding and contracting the ideas they already hold, substituting new for old. It is almost as though the societies themselves could be similarly thought of as extensions of one another, and thus, so to speak, in inevitable disproportion.

If so, we could envisage Highlands peoples as in a constant process of self-substitution, eclipsing or turning one kind of world into another, through (a series of) historical events — comparability is lost in that eclipse, but a kind of compatibility remains. Analogy remains possible. The turn is, in fact, one that the anthropologist routinely replicates when he or she writes on one society with a further society in mind. Thus one might think about Gimi (say) or other peoples in the Eastern Highlands from a Western Highlands' perspective.

To consider Hagen with my ethnographic knowledge of Gimi in mind, I would be writing about political life rather than intiation ceremonies, about the clans that men contrive, not their cults; about the speeches they make, not the flutes they blow. These Hagen practices are connected to what people do elsewhere in their cults but do not take that form. They take their own form; Hagen men produce their own sense of a male collective life that must be kept apart from domestic affairs. But, then, to make an analytical problem from (say) the relationship between political and domestic activity would be to follow a lead initially given by Hagen preoccupations. It is not a problem that somehow takes place between societies; nor could one presume to find its counterpart over the Mt. Hagen range or at the other end of the Wahgi valley, or if one did presume that it would be of proportionate significance. Indeed, one is likely to find that the problem is elsewhere trivialized, or blown up or blown away. Starting with a Hagen preoccupation one could only see how far it could be extended for other societies. Yet the Hagen problem, so to speak, was not simply given by the conditions of life there: its formulation was engineered by my being able to hold other positions and perspectives. I started out also "with Gimi in mind"; thinking about initiation practices, in the Eastern Highlands especially, has without any doubt affected how I would now write about Hagen sociality.

It is possible to leave the origins of such thoughts behind. The debate or conversation that extends each participant beyond the position he or she occupies can conceal the historical process. Knowing there are gaps in one's thoughts becomes at once a pointer to and a cover for what is to be no longer recalled (see Battaglia 1990). Indeed, one might rather fancifully put it that people in general know where they are because they know that they (their ideas) have come from somewhere else now necessarily 'forgotten'.

At the end, then, Tyler's image of the writing anthropologist is turned inside out. In place of the traveller whose composite experience integrates a miscellany of events and locations, I have substituted a cyborg. The anthropologist's writings form a kind of integrated circuit between parts that work as extensions of another. As a field of extensions, the cyborg moves without travelling, as one might imagine the effect of jumping in one's thoughts from one Highlands society to another, or from one aspect of social life to another. The circuit still seems centered, however, on the perceptual tools of the anthropologist.

II. PARTIAL CONNECTIONS

Plates 35 and 36 from Schmitz's **Wantoat** (1963): dance-shields with 'face-designs'of spirits carried by Pasum women and a man. Those carried by the women are made to slide up and down, after the movement of spirits; that by the man represents a bamboo divinity. They are all fringed by bird feathers.

P.1. CULTURES

P.1. FULL OF TREES, FULL OF FLUTES

P.1. TREES

<u>P.1. In the Perpendicular</u>. The inhabitants of the Wantoat Valley on the Huon Peninsula of Papua New Guinea live in a region neither really montane nor coastal. The mountains, high and formidable, run only some ten miles inland from the shoreline. Wantoat people are rain forest cultivators, growing among other things yams cultivated for their length. Pigs are relatively insignificant: wild pigs are rare and keeping domestic ones is described by their ethnographer as "an accessory activity" (Schmitz 1963:27).

Only by the conventions of a kind of division of labor between ethnographers does this area seem to share features both with other coastal regions in the country and with the inland valleys that have appropriated the epithet 'Highlands'. (Cf. J. Weiner ed. 1988; Don Gardner (1983) in turn appropriates a highlands: lowlands distinction to differentiate members of the tiny Mianmin population among the Mountain Ok.) Carl Schmitz calls the Wantoat people and their neighbors Mountain Papuans. Religion and art is the center of interest in the volume (1963) that goes under their name. Wantoat people mount spectacular festivals, introduced by the author with the brief negative statement that, unlike festivals typical of the central Highlands, these do not focus on pigs, either for killing or for exchange. We gather that people's preoccupation is with the growth and fertility of gardens.

A significant dimension to the dances Wantoat people put on at the time of their great festivals is magnitude. Performers literally magnify themselves. They wear barkcloth and bamboo extensions that Schmitz sometimes calls dance-shields, except that in addition to flat surfaces they may also take the shape of cocoons or huge helmets or circles or entire bodies such as the effigy of a cassowary. They are carried by being tied on to the body of the dancer. Given their regular decoration with face designs, a more appropriate generic might be to call these extension 'figures'. The figures that enlarge the body may themselves be enlarged by feathers attached to their perimeter.

In some cases, such figures triple the dancer's height — supported from chest and back, the huge assemblage waves above, twice the size of the man himself. The whole edifice gives the appearance of a tree with a man at its base. The bark-covered frames are, in fact, made out of tall bamboo poles, and at the same time as the bamboos are cut for the individual man, a number of actual trees are cut in order to construct a huge scaffolding in the center of the village.

> The bamboo poles the men tie to their backs are usually some 18 or 20 metres tall. These tremendous swaying poles have to be carefully prepared, and also the festival site must be provided with a construction to support them

> [they are leant here when not being worn] . . .

> Several days before the festival, the men go into the
> woods and cut down the trunks of certain trees whose
> bark has a whitish shine. One evening the post-holes are
> dug, and at night, when women and children are asleep,
> the men hurry back into the forest and fetch the tree-
> trunks, which they set up the same night without a sound.
> In the morning, when everyone wakes up, the scaffolding
> is seen standing . . . as if the spirits had set it there (Schmitz
> 1963:88).

What is true of the tall construction is true for the accompanying dance.
As they make themselves into 'trees', the dancers also make themselves
into 'spirits'. 'Trees' are not the only form in which spirits can appear,
though the cloth and frame are invatiably made out of tree and bamboo
materials. The painted designs on the barkcloth themselves impart a special
atmosphere or power to the figures, and the 'faces' sometimes refer to
specific named deities, such as the deity of all bamboos. Two such figures
are depicted in the frontispiece to this section. They do not, however,
come from Wantoat proper: Schmitz extended his investigations by a visit
to the neighboring people of Pasum, some three days walk to the east
in the upper reaches of the Ramu, where both boys and girls are initiated.
Here, women as well as men may appear under the huge effigies. Whereas
the men's give the appearance of tall trunk-like creatures with a face —
eyes and mouth — at the head, the photograph of two women shows them
holding free-standing eyes and mouths far above their own heads. The
man's figure embeds what the women's appear to have cut out. All are
designed to sway and move.

These particular figures are presented to the Pasum initiates after they
have been forced to spend all night sitting painfully close to a huge fire
that makes them run with sweat. Schmitz (1963:108) explains that the event
is linked with a mythical episode in which an old man caused a bamboo
to produce people. (It is through the Wantoat version of the myth that
he accounts for the Pasum imagery.)

> In those primordial times an old man and his grandson
> lived alone . . . One day the old man told the boy to
> go to a particular tree and lie in wait to shoot a pigeon
> . . . [There were many birds on the tree, but the boy]
> waited patiently until the pigeon described by the old
> man was in the right position for a shot. He took aim
> and let the bow-string fly, and the arrow struck the pigeon
> exactly in the breast . . .

Now the old man, after the boy had gone, had changed himself into this self-same pigeon. When the boy went to pick up the bird, he changed back into his human form. There he stood in front of the lad . . . with the arrow sticking deep in his breast. At every breath the shaft moved gently to and fro. The boy reproached himself bitterly, but the old man soothed him. He instructed him to fetch a long piece of every kind of bamboo, and bring it into their living hut . . .

Now at last the boy was allowed to draw out the arrow from the breast of the old man. At once a strong jet of deep red blood spouted from the wound. Together they filled the lengths of bamboo with the old man's blood. Miraculously, the wound stopped bleeding at the very moment when all the pieces of bamboo were filled to the brim. The two sat down exhausted, and the old man lit a fire. More and more powerfully he blew upon the glowing tinder, till it burst into great flames and the heat became unbearable . . . The sweat ran down in streams over their bare skin, and they suffered hellish torments. Then suddenly the lengths of bamboo burst with a deafening report. At the foot of each piece of bamboo stood a naked man and a naked woman — the first people. Naked, damp and red with the blood out of which they had taken shape, they stood at the foot of the towering bamboo (1963:58-59).

The picture of the bamboo that with a loud retort opens to reveal the people inside holds the attention. If one looks at the dancer with the tall effigy [Frontispiece] one can see him and his towering figure like an entire tree, or see him as attached to/detached from the waving bamboo above, and in that sense created or revealed by it. It should be added that the denotation of the dancers with figures as themselves trees/bamboos is mine. Schmitz does not say as much.[41] And I would not focus attention so on the trees if it were not for the way they evoke for me another set of images, from a quite different part of Papua New Guinea, the Austronesion-speaking archipelago of the Massim. Here, too, we encounter trees full of people.

P.2. A Horizontal Turn. Quite literally, the trees I have in mind are canoes — each hull fashioned from a single trunk — that hold men as they travel across the seas on wealth-hunting expeditions. The trees are mobile in another sense, then, carrying men inside rather that being carried on their backs. Instead of being brought to a center place for display, they radiate out to the peripheries of men's diverse *kula* partnerships: they thus bring back 'more' people, for the sailors return home with the wealth of others.

There is a further social dimension to the vessel. The association of the canoe with a collectivity such as a descent group, and its journeyings as a visible extension of group renown, is well documented for the Massim. In her study of Gawa, for instance, Nancy Munn (1986) makes it clear that the canoe conveys the descent group's prestige as it conveys the prestige of individual crew members. Each man is magnified by his travel overseas, extended and increased by his relationships. Each time, however, he returns to the center, to the descent group with its fixed land and firm ground, on which the trees grow and from which they can be cut and detached.

The decorated canoe that goes overseas is thought of as a ceremonially arrayed person, a beautiful young man. This figure is produced out of materials that were, in mythic times, provided by a woman. It is a woman who first revealed to men how they must make the canoe, and make it into a mobile, swift vessel for travel. She indicated the appropriate red trees by smearing them with her bodily fluids. Until that point, the mythic men were trying to hack a canoe out of garden land itself (Munn 1986:139).[42]

Munn draws a specific connection between canoes, the human body and body decor. The wooden materials are metaphorically identified with internal bodily fluids. "The most marked connection is . . . between the red wood . . . of the hull and blood, which is the body's maternal component and the essential medium from which Gawans say the fetus is formed" (1986:138; Gawan terms omitted). The visual image of this medium is thus present all around in the living trees from which canoes are carved. The process of canoe-making emphasizes the creation of a hollow container. Blood is "in effect, the material out of which the fetus is made" (1986:140) and comes from the mother's body in the same way as the ingredients of the first canoe mythically came from a woman, but the chief property of blood is its interior location. Although Gawans say that the mother's blood coagulates within her to form the child, perhaps the canoe image also invites us to imagine the blood in the form of the interior maternal body itself, its cavity filled by the as-yet unborn children of the descent group.

Canoes are collectively owned by the descent group, though the crews that sail in them are varied. Indeed, it is mandatory that canoes circulate in affinal exchanges, so that the 'children' (the crew) borne by these containers are always more than simply descent group members — they also have an identity through affinal and other connections. Indeed, it is these connections which make the vessel travel.

While there are many children within the canoe — a canoe is sometimes called 'mother' because of the produce it carries in its interior (1986:147) — the entire vessel itself may be treated as a single person, and here of course one has to imagine that single vessel in the company of others when it sails. By analogy with the maternal body and fetus, one may even suggest a further relationship between the internal children-to-be who will fill the container, and the child made visible as a matter of external form. For the canoe itself 'appears' as a result of the actions which men perform on the outside of the hull. It is decorated (carved, painted and ornamented) on its exterior, and an outrigger made from a type of white wood associated with masculinity. The red wood is also covered with whitewash, so that it is concealed beneath this painted exterior. The canoe's surface evokes the individuating and paternal facial appearance of persons, which connects each person to his/her kin outside the descent group. Thus the carving and decorating of the canoe is done so that the canoe will travel away from the land where the trees grew, in order to effect exchanges with persons from other lands.

Now I implied a contrast between the potential plurality of the (invisible) persons who would fill up the canoe, and the conversion of the canoe into a single (visible) person when conceived as an object from the outside sailing in a company. If so, then 'one' child is also 'many' children, depending on one's internal or external perspective. Consequently a single person — thought of as a descent group or a canoe — in effect comprises a plurality of persons, and the internal diversity of the descent group can be perceived as a unity from the outside perspective of other kin. The one form (canoe, mother) contains many forms of itself within, even as many trees grow on the one territory. The canoe is not only a young man, but also both mother and child.

In a converse set of images, Gawans draw analogies between garden growth and bodily reproduction (cf. Mun 1986:296, n. 29). A garden forms a mass like a woman's body, may be said to give birth, and members of a descent group are referred to as its 'plantings'. Elsewhere in the Massim, explicit parallels are made between yams in the ground and the growing child in a woman's body; what is crucial here is that what is contained must remain hidden till the moment of birth, for only thus will it grow. The land must be heavy, Gawans say (1986:86) in order to bear, and further aesthetic practices concern the respective heaviness of the land and lightness of the people who feed from it. Indeed, the equation between growth and what is hidden is so strong that Gawans prefer contemplating food to consuming it. Food growing in the land satiates personal bodily hunger, for to consume food is to increase the possibility of hunger. There is thus an intimate connection between what is visible to the eye — the external form of the swelling gardens — and what is invisible, to the point that people derive internal bodily satisfaction, satiation, from their perception of plentiful food still growing within. The full garden is, so to speak, an unexcavated version of the full belly. It is the completer, and more satiating, image.

Gawans have introduced us to what in English would be a quantitative paradox. If 'one' contains 'many' then one is also a version of many, epitomized in the recapitulation of descent group members as one. It is worth adding that the bonds between these members (1986:27) are those of land and blood, and that in terms of bodily composition, members recapitulate the bonding itself. Each member contains the group. At the same time, in terms of the capacity for making extensions and connections, each member potentially belongs to a matrix of radiating relations.

The tree works as a double image, at once the container of persons (the canoe and the crew), and the person that is carried (the fetus carried in the cavity of the descent group/mother). The point is replicated in fine detail in the very valuables carried by the crew, to which people through their spells and magic strive to convey the quality of motion itself (Munn 1983).

Debbora Battaglia's (1983) analysis of the anthropomorphic connotations of the shell necklaces exchanged by Sabarl islanders, to the far southeast of Gawa, augments the point. Sabarl men journeying across the seas, finding their exchange partners, carry in their hands replicas of a person that contains movement within him/itself. The back and forth movement of the journey is inscribed in the intertwined red and white strands of the necklace.

> The strands are divided into an 'out' and 'back' side by a clasp that symbolically 'turns' the flow of the valuable shell discs 'back towards home' . . [They merge in a] 'head' which transforms the necklace from a married woman's ornament into a ceremonial valuable. A necklace with a head is aid to acquire a 'voice' in the form of shell chimes. It is the head that makes the object 'more like people' (1983:300, Sabarl terms omitted).[43]

The image both speaks and moves, and journeying is thus contained within it, even as the reciprocal relationship of partners is contained within the gift transaction, and the cumulative history of back and forth transactions is contained within the fame of the descent group. Thus we see persons either as people produced by their descent group and ferried by its vessels, or as the relationships of which they are composed and by which they extend themselves, in the same way as Wantoat dancers emerge from and merge into the faces of the spirit out of whom they once all came.

I have drawn these examples not just from northern and eastern Papua New Guinea, but from quite divergent and random social-historical circumstances — Wantoat here, Pasum there; Gawa, Sabarl — and from items built for particular occasions to durable vessels, from myth to conception ideology. The only connections seem my free associations. Yet those seem bound to be tripped up on the very issue of association: how one knows in each instance what one is 'looking at'.

P.2. FLUTES

P.1. An Impasse of Imagery. Before the issue of connections, then, there is another. What kinds of **forms** are these perceived to be? If we ignore the little details about color, forget that canoes also sail with mouth and eyes at their prows or that one of the remarked-upon features of the tall bamboo poles is their capacity to move and sway above the head of the speaker, one could argue that all that connects Wantoat effigies and Gawan canoes are highly generalized and accessible resemblances. 'Head' and 'eyes' and 'body' are visuals that one might expect any people anywhere to draw upon. So why should one even think of joining them as though in comparison?

One thinks of comparisons because other people do. For example, one may think of the comparisons of exchange systems implicit in the collection of essays on the *kula* (Leach and Leach 1983). Or one may think of Gilbert Herdt's (1984) examination of ritualized homosexual practices across Papua New Guinea and Irian Jaya, which incorporate some of the elements touched on above, such as initiation, the creation of new persons, the enclosure of men and their release; and so forth. Gifts, festivals, initiation rituals, sexual practices: this is a scale of phenomena anthropologists are used to taking for comparison. We are also used to taking other scales such as individual objects or items of paraphernalia, and indeed here our confidence often extends to distribution maps. Thus Kenneth Gourlay (1975) had tracked and plotted the distribution (for 233 societies or places or areas throughout Papua New Guinea) of different types of sound-producing instruments, including bullroarers. These latter instruments are rather like miniaturized versions of some of the Wantoat figures, elongated, often inscribed with facial markings, the habitat of spirits, and found in northern Australia as well as Irian Jaya and much of Papua New Guinea, bar the Highlands and the Massim.

Just to 'look at', these oval elongated forms could as well be Papuan Gulf ancestor boards as Highlands fighting shields. But to think of the Wantoat figures as aerophones moves comparison in certain directions. The origin of human beings was after all the bamboo that split open with a loud retort, a 'tree' that made a noise. Perhaps one would not think of trees as aerophones in themselves, unless, that is, one had heard the late afternoon wind through the tops of casuarinas, or recalled the birds that flock to fruiting species like so many feathers round the perimeter of a bark and bamboo plaque. When men present themselves as spirits in the form of birds (e.g. Feld 1982), their songs are also bird song. And elsewhere trees are hollowed precisely in order to produce sound — from the huge slit-gongs that lie horizontally in Sepik men's houses or the sturdy hourglass drums held by Highlands dancers as they bob up and down in rhythm, to the miniature instruments Trobriand youths hold when they dance for tourist parties, and sell afterwards.

Gourlay restricts his own investigations to a three-way survey of bullroarers, slit-gongs and sacred flutes, a scale that apparently satisfies the methodological requirement of comparing like with like.[44] Clearly, however, even on the basis of investigating sound-producing instruments, the comparisons that Papua New Guinean imagery suggest would exceed these dimensions. The notes emitted from such enclosed spaces evoke, for instance, sounds that come from behind masks or the voices of spirits (Tuzin 1980:56-57) from inside houses or beyond fences. Gourlay provides ample evidence himself for the frequent association of music with ancestral voices and wind with the persons/fetus contained within. But on this scale, these associations simply become the attributes or the 'meaning' of the objects.

We seem to have drawn rather far away from canoes. Ignoring the conch shell that can herald their arrival on shore, or the sibilance of their movement through the water, no one ever thought of classifying canoes as aerophones. Yet those who have canoes may carve their sides with totemic designs the way slit-gongs may be carved (e.g. Gewertz 1983:40); to the casual observer, Trobriand house-roofs look like overturned hulls; and some of the Melanesians who hold initiation rituals make novices emerge from the mouths of monsters in the same way as they emerge from the mouths of men's houses and the wind of spirits is emitted from gongs. People are sometimes quite literal-minded about such connotations. As Gillian Gillison (1980; in press) has reported on several occasions, Gimi flutes are bamboo aerophones explicitly plugged and blown as extensions of the mouth, instruments that release men's spirit and is released as a fetus, evoking the cries of birds, like the child unwrapped from its mother's body and like the mother that gives birth to a tubal womb.

But what are houses, here, and what are trees, and have I not been a bit too naive even about the most obvious visuals? With what certainty do I recognize eyes and mouths on the Wantoat effigies? Indeed, the Wantoat 'faces' that appear to stare at us become not faces at all, if one listens to the disassembling verbal commentary of local speakers.

Schmitz (1963:94f.) analyzes the specific designs of some of these faces according to local exegesis. [See the central face design in Figure 1 on next page.] The human features seem to disappear, as he proceeds, 'the face' absorbed into numerous bodies that appear as separate tiny markings on its surface. Thus he finds[45] **within** the design of the face those hourglass shapes that refer to drums (that people hold in their hands), and enclose whole body cavities between them, while apparent hands are said to be not hands but the outlines of knobbly yam tubers (with which people fill their bodies). Moreover, while for one particular piece persons readily agreed with Schmitz's 'recognition' of eyes and nose, they denied that the opened band beneath was a mouth. Spirits, he was told, did not have mouths. He had to go to Pasum to find people who denoted these lower cavities as mouths.

FIGURE 1

From **Wantoat** 1963: plate 14, 15, 16.

SCHMITZ'S DRUMS

'Dance shields' from Wantoat.
1 and 2 are said to have 'face designs';
1 to be a 'yam design'

FACES   YAMS

Yet am I not being naive in turn? Surely we do not have to decide what the forms are? Symbolic analysis shows us readily enough that any one item can 'mean' many things to many persons on many occasions. All I am doing in these endless potential analogies is collecting meanings and, of course, no one dreams of comparing meanings: an anthropologist compares the practice and use of meaning-making. One does not delimit potential analogies but documents the analogies people draw. A few levels and contexts is surely all one needs to escape from this pseudo-Frazerian pastiche.

P.2. Levels and Contexts. But levels and contexts have to be identified also. One might define initiation practices as a set of social 'contexts', or find a 'level' of explanation as Gourlay, for instance, proposes when he establishes male-female relations as the significant domain reflected in dominant themes accompanying his symbolic analysis (1975:94). Frequently one tries to marry two different orders of phenomena so that each provides a context and grounding for the other. It is in this vein that Terence Hays (1986,1988) embarked on his meticulous and thoughtful survey of 'the sacred flute complex' in the Highlands of Papua New Guinea. He makes it clear that he is not simply itemizing a part of the material culture, but also investigating its significance in relation to ideas about growth and fertility. Hays's intention is to identify

> certain themes . . . which not only link together a large
> number of Highlands societies, but also suggest historical
> connections with other cults involving wind instruments
> in New Guinea. . . [and from] these common themes,
> to establish a comparative base from which other analyses
> can proceed (1986:435).

Across the Highlands bamboo flutes turn up time and again as the focus of ritual treatment, above all in male initiation. More than that, Hays shows that they are almost everywhere accompanied by very similar stories about how the tubes were once women's appendages, since stolen by men. With men's theft came men's power, specifically reproductive power and control over the growth and fertility of persons. The flutes are now a secret that men hold apart from women. As one travels from society to society, one encounters similar suppositions; whether the flutes emit the cries of birds, or ancestors, or children, blown by men they are able to evoke this power (Gewertz ed. 1988).

It is clear there are connections; the correspondencies which Hays documents between Highlands societies are too close to be dismissed. It is also clear, as Roger Keesing (1982:35) notes, that these do not comprise a multitude of independent inventions; if anything, they compose a kind of conventional repertoire. It is tempting to take the further step and suppose a regional culture, every society presenting a variation on the same theme. Hays wishes to elucidate just such 'common themes': the continuities in the power Highlanders ascribe to these instruments, their role in male secret cults, and above all the way they are used to validate men's dominance through the myth of theft. Taking the flute complex as a substrate prompts the analyst to compare, for instance, how it operates as a central focus of lengthy male initiation practices in the Eastern Highlands with its contrasting attenuation in the Western Highlands — including the enigma of a place like Hagen where flute stories of a kind exist but where there are no initiation practices. One is further prompted to look for co-variables to account for the uneven distribution of these practices, and thereby order the various analogies on a common footing. The result would be to produce a scale against which to plot incidence.

Yet the difficulty with this comparison is that our supposed common regional culture is composed of the very features which are the object of study, the 'meanings' people give to these instruments, the analogies they set up. We could say we were dealing with cultures somehow based on an agreed symbolic substratum beyond which all is elaboration. Yet the common cultural core, the themes common to the variations, is not a context or level independent of local usage. Or to put it this way, wherever one looks, the flute is already an image. It never exists in a generic form, only in a multiplicity of specific ones.

For instance, flutes are commonly blown in pairs and, quite apart from the melodies they produce, are invariably designated in anthropomorphic terms. Hays documents the variation. Very often they are described as a male and female couple, but otherwise may be a pair of (male) age-mates or (female) co-wives, or two female spirits (1986:438). As a general comment on anthropological analysis in this area (and not on this particular survey), I observe the following.

One, it is somewhat disconcerting that whether the flutes are male or female or both does not seem to make much difference to the anthropologist's analytical level of male-female relations — which is the perception of the difference that being male or female makes. Along the first dimension the variation seems insignificant, yet is plotted against a dimension that is defined by such variation. Nonetheless, two, the power that is described as an indigenous attribute of the flutes — the effect they have when people hear them — is taken as part of the anthropologist's evidence about the way the deployment of flutes supports men's exercise of power over women. Here is a startling disproportion. In the former case, the 'level' of analysis appears untouched by local constructions of difference; in the second, the 'context' of power relations proves to be originally based on an extrapolation from local concepts.

In fact, the question of contexts and levels folds in on itself in another peculiar way: that what appears in one society as a focus of significance, a key artefact, in another can be 'an accessory activity'. They are not in this sense the same. While it seems that the very presence of flutes at an initiation ceremony is enough to measure their significance, however attenuated the ceremony, there are Highlands societies where initiation-like rituals are practiced but where flutes play no significant role (as in Paiela in the Western Highlands) and others such as Hagen where there is no significant initiation at all.[46] In the Paiela case, it is not too fanciful to see as flutes of a kind the tiny bamboo tubes that bachelors put out to test the spirit woman whose blessing they desire. As the bamboos fill up with water, they indicate her presence. I quote from Aletta Biersack's account (1982:246, emphasis removed):

> The most important aspect of the bamboo rite concerns those boys who have visited the mountain retreat at least once before. These will have left bamboo tubes standing in swampy water. . . and during their recent absence water will have seeped into them. This water then encodes the messages the [spirit] woman would convey more directly were she and her activities visible to the boy. If the water level is high, if the water is clear and if it moves when the boy looks at it, then [she] is thought not to be menstruating and by implication not to be growing the inner skin of the boy. But if the water level is low, reddish rather than clear and not animated, then [she] is thought to be menstruating and by implication not to be growing the inner skin of the boy.
>
> The bamboo tube . . . is the very house the [spirit] woman is domiciled within.

But for Hagen perhaps we are looking in the wrong direction; perhaps better analogies would lie in other ceremonies. What about the pig stakes that are driven into the earth on ceremonial grounds? — the stakes do not 'carry' the pigs, but pigs are tethered to them, a sign of clan productivity before they radiate out to diverse exchange partners. In fact, they almost remind one of the digging sticks[47] in women's hands that make the earth yield the tubers that feed the pigs. But then again, in Hagen at least, the row of stakes on the ceremonial ground indicating past transactions and the future promise of pigs also evokes[48] the tally of shell transactions that men wear on the chest. These comprise tiny slats of bamboo, each gift transaction in shells augmenting it by another bamboo length. Do the visible slats tether invisible shells to them?

Such evocations will not quite do. The pursuit of 'other directions' leaves a sense of there being no one entity to compare between our several Highlands societies; no one set of meanings that will do as a substrate, and no set of contexts or levels for usage to be arranged in a coordinate series. The ordinary flutes that Hagen men play for amusement both are and are not being used like the sacred transverse instruments kept wrapped elsewhere in a men's house or inflicted as tools of coercion on boy initiates. The connections are partial to say the least. And they are partial because there is no base line for analogy in the way they are used. What evocation should we pursue? Find the analog for the coercive flute in the persuasive words that stream out of Hagen men's mouths? Find the analog for the Hagener's entertaining instrument in Gimi gossip and pleasantries? And where do we find the Hagen analog to initiation itself? In men's ceremonial exchange? In women's childbirth practices? For if we cannot abstract some independent set of contexts or levels that will hold across all the cases, then how do we control the analogies we perceive? What tells us a Gimi flute is or is not like the bamboo tallies that Hagen men sport at their throats, or like the secrets that Paiela enclosures keep invisible from women? Or even perhaps like the string bags that Hagen women once wore in an elongated bunch down their backs?

Perhaps the real problem is that the athropologist's contexts and levels of analysis are themselves often at once both part and yet not part of the phenomena s/he hopes to organize with them. Because of the cross-cutting nature of the perspectives they set, one can always be swallowed by another. Sacred flutes are not coterminous with either initiation or fertility rites, and any such context will afford its own specific and non-generic perspective on the material s/he might wish to assemble. And what is a flute? No external criteria can escape contamination by local meanings — whether we regard it as a length of bamboo, a vessel, a sound-making instrument, an artefact with mystical power, or as a male or female appendage. Its attributes can no more be counted than we can perceive 'it' as a single entity set apart from the purposes for which it is made.

My interest is in the proportions that sustain the conviction of anthropological accounts. Yet the examples here seem to have got out of hand. — Out of scale, one could almost say, except that there is a kind of scaling to them.

One obvious intention was to recapitulate points that both Gourlay and Hays themselves observed in their comparative analyses, that the analytical strategy of differentiating levels or putting entities into context already shows that one cannot extract individual items (artefacts, institutions) from a social/cultural matrix and treat them as so many discrete units. There is no automatic scale to be generated from such units. Scales have to be created by the anthropologist, and one is not, after all, content to count sound-producing instruments. But there was also a specific point to the examples I selected. Trees and flutes appear to the Western eye as things intrinsically separate from persons; or rather they are intrinsically separate from the bodies of individual persons. But what we seem to be told by the Melanesians concerned, over and again, whether we look within these things or beyond them, is that the effigies, canoes, stakes or whatever are at once of the person and more than the person. It is not just that they are extensions integral to the relationships a person makes, and 'instruments' in that sense, but that the physical body is apprehended as composed of those instruments as it is composed of relationships. The relations (the instruments) appear intrinsic to the body. They are its features. Each example presents us with a total figuration of that statement. It is not the way anthropologists control the analogies, then, that seems at issue, but the way the actors do.

P.2.   CENTER AND PERIPHERY

P.1. OBVIATION

P.1. Prefigurement. Total figuration can be grasped by narrational strategies already to hand. Most inclusive, perhaps, is what has come to be known as obviational analysis, after Roy Wagner's (e.g. 1986a, 1986b) elucidation of the recursive processual form he calls obviation. Obviation is manifested "as a series of substitutive metaphors that constitute the plot of a myth (or the form of the ritual), in a dialectical movement that closes when it returns to its beginning point" (1986a:xi). Not just myth or ritual but social process in general have been perceived this way. James Weiner makes the point in his monograph on the Foi of the Lake Kutubu area: "what the anthropologist perceives as social process, the flow of events, can perhaps best be rendered in terms of the replacement or substitution of tropes by other tropes" (1988:9). Obviational 'analysis' replicates for the observer the temporal and spatial sequences by which persons move themselves from one position to another through their constant perception and reperception of relations. What at the end is made 'obvious' is the relational basis of their perception.

This form of elucidation, in turn, finds an explicit counterpart in the relational symbolism of societies where sociality is a taken-for-granted background to human intention. Where relations are perceived as immanent in things and persons, people work to make them known through the analogies they reveal. Persons and things are thus decomposed to reveal the relations which constitute them. To the anthropologist, this effort may well create a paradox. Prefigurement would be tantamount to conceiving of a 'society' or 'culture' as already in place, a configuration of which every new person is him or herself a recomposition. Yet such a configuration is suggestively there in the procreative spatial imagery of North Mekeo where any one thing is either the inside or the outside of another (cf. Mosko 1985; also M. Strathern 1989). It is there in the Iqwaye conception of a single original being enclosed on itself, and in the mathematics to which this gives rise. Iqwaye know that one can only ever count fractions of one (Mimica 1988; compare Gillison 1987). We already have the theoretical tools to approach such presumptions about connections and relationships.

It does seem that I had taken a step backwards. The problems posed in the previous section only appeared as such because I was ignoring a whole area of already established anthropological understanding. It is as though I had dropped from my mentality the intervening modes of interpretation by which anthropologists over the last few decades have dealt with symbolic diversity. This was a step backwards not just from obviational analysis but from one of its precursors, structuralism. If obviational analysis can elucidate the prefiguring of social and cultural totalities, structuralist analysis rests on the prefiguring of the elements out of which mental operations are apparently composed. To have overlooked these possibilities, appears in retrospect absurd. Perhaps this 'gap' in my account was created by the scattering effect of the examples.

P.2. Eliciting Forms. Indeed, the examples could have been picked off the dusty shelves of some cataloguing enterprise that anthropology left behind years ago. It is not so much a question of the correspondencies seeming meaningless or false as of their seeming unlocated. They need to be placed in order to tell us something of the way Papua New Guineans or other Melanesians (as cultural actors) manage connections.

There is surely a **specificity** to the movement Melanesians perceive, to the journeys these actors take. They are not random cosmopolitans, heady with the world's cultures, tasting this here or that there. They travel with cultural intent, like the overseas *kula* voyagers who go to identified islands and individual exchange partners for famed shell valuables, or like the dancer whose power to keep a massive bamboo edifice above his head from breaking his neck comes from the power of the image he presents to others, the named spirit they see in the single movement of man and figure. These are not casual journeys or gestures without risk. They are oriented towards very specific effects: relations have to be made known. What is present and presented in a specific situation is intended to elicit a specific response from a partner, recognition from an audience.

The response may inhere in the anticipated, indeed sometimes prescribed, reactions of persons. It may also be staged. The effect that an image creates can be presented as a further image; one figure is seen to 'produce' a counter-figure. What we commonly perceive as the social context of a performance or ritual may well be composed of a series of figures and counter-figures, like a series of tropes, each as precisely presented as the last and as though elicited by it. We could think of such elicitation as prefigured evocations: not an open-ended journeying but anticipated destinations.

The previous section with its 'problems', then, was by contrast an exercise in unanticipated evocation, apparently losing all sense of proportion in pursuing images that appeared at once too general and too particular to organize analytical attention. The narrational suggestion of resemblance between trees and flutes simply set in motion a train of isolated correspondencies — between what can be hollowed out and what can be carved, between what is cut and what grows or stands for growth or what seems to grow with a cavity, between what emits noise by being beaten on its exterior and what emits noise form its interior, and so forth. The resemblances seem artificial because they are being made by the narrative. This in turn is because the narrative cannot do what Melanesians do in taking similarity or resemblance — the relations between things — for granted. Against such a background of resemblances, the "moral foundation of human action" becomes for them the making of distinctions (J. Weiner 1988:9). If in imitation one were to foreground the transformational and differentiating sequences by which forms appear in specific succession, the arbitrary nature of these correspondencies will perhaps disappear.

The Wantoat and Pasum figures which I evoked are among numerous masked and figured forms — apart from the man who is the tree and is at the base of the tree, men are also figured crouching under the skirts of cassowaries or carrying a huge round nest on the head or framed by moon-shaped crests. These are not random figurations but, like the succession of forms that appear at the Umeda and Yafar rites of growth in the West Sepik (Gell 1975; Juillerat in press), occur in identifiable sequence and to differentiating effect.

The anthropologist's business, then, has to be the specific evocations that work for those who produce such images. S/he must attend to what people make explicit. Particular moments or forms give rise to or are displaced by others. One witnesses, so to speak, how images create images,[49] as in the effect of how one kind of masked dancer gives way to another, or in the perspectives that separate the moment when a bamboo flute is being treated as a container from the moment when what is important is that it is wrapped up and being carried in a string bag. As with all these ideas, people use images as extensions of other images. Any number of meanings are possible. An image "**contains** or **elicits** them all, and all that is necessary is to retain the image itself" (Wagner 1986b:xv, original emphasis). If what is contained is made known through what is elicited or evoked, the elucidation of meaning is positioned on usage.

A performance or a temporal sequence, such as actors create in the procreative movement from betrothal gifts to bridewealth to child payments or in the oscillation of ceremonial exchange where now one partner and now the other is the donor, would thus provide an analogical frame for the creativity of imagery itself. A sense of growth and movement comes from the way one set of values is both displaced by and 'produces' (makes appear) its successor, as Munn observes of Gawa, when she talks of female potency being converted into individually memorable artefacts such as shell armbands and necklaces (1986:145), or of a feather headdress, materially extending the body of a dancer, being seen as a metaphor for the *kula* necklace that will extend his fame as a person (1983:287). To reveal the analogy, to reveal an internal relation between similarity and difference, is like revealing a prior position, a figure which has been displaced. To follow such a path, the anthropologist would then be following through deliberate substitutions as they occur within a sequence of practices. I have indicated that there are some fine analyses to hand in contemporary Melanesian studies. We would be deceived, however, to think they afforded a self-sufficient dimension, as though they were simply completing the prefigured world which Melanesians take as their starting point. Melanesians use movement between persons to decompose their world.

One of my present purposes is to show the way anthropologists' activities constantly create 'remainders' for themselves, starting points for apparently new but not quite independent dimensions. I therefore do indeed take a step backwards, and from Hays' position ask how we can deploy such insights and yet avoid the kind of exclusive focus on single cultures his comparative overview also sought to avoid.

P.2.   COMMUNICATION

P.1.   Complex Knowledge.   While the idea of a sequence is an apposite image for the analyst's journey of discovery, and while succession and revelation are certainly explicit in Melanesian myths, rituals and not least their exchange relationships, events do not simply carry people forward. Richard Werbner (1989) underlines the point during the course of his re-analysis of West Sepik material.

He recapitulates the sequencing of events at the Umeda *ida* festival described by Alfred Gell (1975), though takes up an explicit position on figures which Gell treated only incidentally. Here we encounter forms not unlike the Wantoat effigies — figures extended by other figures, now encased in massive structures, now elongated with feathers. Gell's own analysis had established the significance of dialectical juxtaposition, the following of one design by another, to the point of observing that "one rapidly arrives at the idea that there are not **many** ritual figures, but basically only **one** such figure in process of transformation" (1975:296, original emphasis). The observation is matched by Werbner's foregrounding of an apparently unimportant preliminary act (an enactment of birth) which recapitulates and anticipates the outcome of the diverse actions that follow (1989:150). Time is thus contained in that moment, that opening gesture a figuration of the whole.

The masks with their frames, coverings, fringes and plumes, making their appearance to the accompaniment of wooden trumpets (Gell 1975:158), are composed of products associated with trees and plants. Umeda exegesis of the whole figuration of the man and his mask[50] draws a clear parallel between tree structure and the structure of the body, in the case of the cassowary mask with a band of fruit at the top like the daughters men give away in marriage (1975:237, 241). Now from the viewpoint of any one hamlet, others are divided into hamlets with whom daughters are exchanged and hamlets with whom masks are exchanged.[51] From one man's point of view, it is thus possible to wear the masks of other men from other communities, provided one does not marry their daughters (1975:52).

Werbner opens out this act of exchange as the centerpiece of his own spatial analysis. As we discover, space like time also folds back on itself in oscillating center-periphery relations. People dispersed in their bush settlements congregate at times of the festival in their villages; and disperse again. More than that, the centers they create are seen to have analogs in other people's centers, spaced out on their social peripheries. The data are complex and I render part of his argument verbatim [original paragraphing ignored].

> By masking, a man effects a symbolic transition across time through space. Inside the mask he enters the inner space from which life came at the beginning of time — one tree or another, according to the origin of a primordial being — and thus reversing space and time, he himself becomes a primordial being, such as the Cassowary.
>
> Men who are outsiders to each other's territory exchange masks. In this way they turn themselves into insiders and thereby gain access to each other's inner space. For most of . . . the year, they spend their lives virtually contained within contiguous strips of land . . . During the festival, however, they expand their limits . . .There the men create perpetual contact between their hamlets, by means of the masks and women . . . The women, like the masks, are containers for the men as insiders, although each container is restricted to its own insiders. The mask is the male womb, the woman the female womb (1989:156, footnotes omitted).
>
> In terms of social exchange, territory and women are treated as antithetical providers and containers of the space of life, territory being immovable and women movable. Reciprocity over and exchange of a life-space container brings people into physical contact. And people can reconfigure their physical environment, the immovable surroundings, by their selection of the movable containers of life space . . . On the one hand, the mask, like a woman, is movable and on the other, like a territory, it relates to permanence. By sharing access to the space within masks, [men] establish a higher order of symbolic contact between territories that do not exchange women (1989:195-6).

The details would be out of proportion here, but Werbner maps the geographical disposition of Umeda and the other communities (villages, hamlets) in its vicinity in order to display the relationships of exchange between them. He argues that they evince the operation of two principles. One is that society is represented as a simple binary unit, by which he refers to moiety and other dyadic relations not mentioned here; and second that each community sees itself at the center of a universe of communities (1989:218). A man does not simply place himself at the center of his own network; rather men are placed *vis-à-vis* **other men's** centers. Thus, for example, the village of Punda is, from the Umeda perspective, a kind of mirror version of Umeda (1989:213), external perpetual exchange across this pair of villages forming a greater community according to rules of contact between non-adjacent territories. Each is 'another man's center' to the other.

Punda has a pivotal place in Werbner's theorizing about regional communications. It is mirror to Umeda but no duplicate, for it has its own character. The same village is also in contact with communities of the neighboring Amanab language. This area includes Yafar village, the subject of Juillerat's ethnography (1986; in press). Punda intermarry with both Umeda and Yafar; like Punda, Yafar borrowed the fertility cult *ida* from Umeda, which they call *yangis*. Umeda is regarded as the 'mother' to its Punda and Yafar 'daughters'.

In a provocative approach to the apparently uneven distribution of knowledge about one another's cult practices, Werbner (in press) suggests that the difference between the Umeda *ida* and the Yafar *yangis* can be understood from the Yafar point of view both in terms of the view they hold of themselves in relation to Umeda **and** in terms of a recentering of the practices for themselves. Yafar openly acknowledge having borrowed the *yangis* from outside: to them it is exotic, whereas for Umeda it is indigenous. It is a fruit of Umeda culture, one might say, that nurtures them. At the same time, Yafar have recentered the cult, ensuring that it does indeed nurture them. As Werbner observes, *yangis* cannot replicate *ida*. Both communities perform their rituals for the same desired outcome (fertility); but the 'daughter's' view is not the 'mother's', no empty metaphor this but a summary of several dimensions along which Yafar reconstruct the view from having been born rather than the view from giving birth.

Werbner's analysis provides a model for imagining the way people interpret one another's rituals, creating their own centers to view a world that they know consists of other people's centers. The view, those centers, is conserved. Communities are in communication with one another, but do not force their own perspectives on the perspectives of others. Each establishes its own version. The practices of a neighboring community thus elicit a counter-practice that is neither its dialectical product nor genetic derivative. Communication is effective, the circuit so to speak operates, but the 'messages' are only partially transferred.

This model was originally derived from a single language area, but can be extended across the two language areas where Umeda and Yafar are situated. An inspiration for Werbner's analysis was the pulsating movement of the Umeda festivals themselves. Communities expand and scatter again as, gathered in from their dispersed gardens, people become momentarily conscious both of their own centrality and of the necessity to maintain relations with other centers on their periphery — a contraction and expansion of focus. That contraction and expansion is mirrored in the way individual men decorate to expand themselves and then shrink to human size afterwards. However, the scale on which Werbner sees this must always remain the view from the center. The view from the periphery is another view from the center, a version composed of the diverse named communities brought into communication with one another through men's efforts in ritual congregation and outward exchange. The view can, as we have seen, cross language groups. What is at issue for these Western Lowlanders is the further possibility of making one's own interior out of the interiors of persons centered elsewhere, of 'borrowing' culture.

The pulsation between center and periphery that links but does not encompass or exhaust the differences between communities appears to work for a relatively circumscribed local region. Yet it works in a kind of retrospective manner, like the overview of a villager describing the after-effects of past communication between villages, a ripple effect of the kind that *kula* partners envisage when they think of the partners of their partners. Would one be resorting to an inappropriate metaphor to suggest there was anything comparable to such communication once one left the orbit of neighbors and the neighbors of neighbors? What about the Mountain Ok area, for instance, with its population spread over several different languages?

Barth's analysis of six related language communities poses an interesting counterposition in this regard. Here, religious beliefs and practices appear to vary enormously. By contrast, house types and dress "are so similar that, apart from a few indicative details, photographs from one village could be used to illustrate life in another" (1987: 2). But let us look at one example of a tiny indicative difference in dress, at an item that itself depicts a pulsating movement.

P.2. Export and Import. One of Werbner's criticisms of Gell's own analysis of the *ida* is that we are witnessing not simply the unfolding of a single sequence (a single transformation), but the merging and intertwining of sequences that are split from the moment of their inception. He points out that Gell dwells on the cassowary figure that appears at the beginning of the performance, but in fact the cassowary (Cassowary of the Mothers) is only one of two figures, the other being Fish of the Daughters (1989:167). By restoring the importance of this, and of the clowns whom Gell also relegates to one side, Werbner produces analytical coordinates for his own theorizing of dual organization. Similarly, from a Yafar perspective, he (in press) shows how a pair of primal figures turn out to be male and female in the 'same' (one) male form. The point is explicit in J. Weiner's (1988:142) obviational analysis of the conventional separation of men and women transformed into the opposition between male cross cousins figuratively male and female to one another. I could put this another way. It would be possible to start with a complete or total figuration whatever the number, whether with one **or** with two. That is, the starting point could be either a single figure or a figure perceived as split into two — as in the duo of masks that first appear in the *ida.*

For either 'one' or 'two' can be seen as an expansion or contraction of the other (one as an encompassment of two which is a doubled one; or two as a division of one which is half a two). The image of pulsation I now evoke could almost be taken as a play on this arithmetic that is not quite arithmetic. By contrast with Wantoat effigies out of which a man's body appears, or the heavy, neck-breaking (Gell 1975:240) Umeda masks that appear to engulf head and torso, it belongs to a version of the widespread and mundane netbag (strictly, looped string bag). I take my observations from Maureen Mackenzie's (1986; in press) analysis of the Telefol string bag and of its relation to similar artefacts found all over the Mountain Ok area. As she says at the beginning of her article (in press):

> [p]erhaps the most striking use of the string bag, and that which has attracted the analytic attention of Melanesianists, is its use as a baby's cradle. Hanging from the mother's head like a possum's pouch (Gell 1975:142-3), the type of loosely looped bag has the same potential for expansion as the uterus. Reflecting a visual and functional similarity to an external womb it stretches and swells to contain and protect the fruits of garden and womb.

It is appropriate that the initial image is a female one, since everywhere such bags are made by women, and wherever they are part of the cultural repertoire are worn by women. In some parts, they are also worn by men. This is true for Telefol and Umeda. In the marvellous passage to which Mackenzie refers, Gell describes how a man and his bag ('bilum') are as inseparable as a man and his dog, containing his most personal possessions, a kind of shadow spirit. But if so, then the woman's swollen bag, a larger version of the man's, evinces her public role 'in society' and a most material presence.

> [A woman] is not really 'dressed' unless her woman's bilum. . . is suspended over her back. And if a man's

bilum contains his personality in the form of magical
materials, still more so does a women's swollen . . . bilum
express her role in society, since it is filled with food
(the nourisher) and/or with offspring (the child-bearer)
(Gell 1975:143).

Of course, isolating 'the string bag' is neither more nor less respectable
a computational step than isolating 'the sacred flute.' It is not a single
entity. Should one think of the distinctive looping technique, for instance,
one discovers it is used equally for making men's hair coverings. At various
times both Umeda and Telefol men wear penis gourds — but elsewhere
in Papua New Guinea, such as the central Highlands where men do not
ornament their personality in this way, women loop pubic aprons for men
by the same techniques. (Mackenzie (1986) also illustrates fish nets, cloaks
and body armor from other parts of the country.) Should, however, one
think of these bags as containers, one might be lured into making comparisons
with basket-weave fish traps or the mosquito bags which enclose people
in the Middle Sepik when they sleep. However, for Telefol, and for the
Mountain Ok region in general, Mackenzie draws the reader's attention
to a specific internal contrast between string bags as items of men's and
of women's dress.

The pulsating image of the bag is apt for either sex. Over a women's
back, the string bag hangs slack or swells with produce according to the
periodicity of its fruition. Its contours thus reveal the presence of something
inside, and the contained items give it shape. This internal pulsation is
replicated as a movement between persons. From the outside a women's
bag is plain — it hangs down her entire back unadorned. The bags that
men wear over their necks and shoulders are, by contrast, elaborately
enlarged, enhanced by decorations of bird feathers, different designs
indicating different initiatory stages. The magnification and growth of men
is thus carried as a kind of exterior skin to their bodies. It is important
to appreciate Mackenzie's point that such bags denote a dual social origin.
There would be no frame on which men could fasten the feathers if there
were no women to loop the bags for them; and nothing for women to
put in their bags if there were no men to fill them.[52] There has, so to
speak, to be communication between men and women before anything
is produced in the world with which to communicate.

While there is evident interdependence of form between men's and
women's bags, one of these two types comprises a recapitulation of the
two. The male bag contains both male and female forms — indeed the
elaboration of bags beyond the principal 'female' form is an exclusive 'male'
activity. Moreover, men's bags undergo transformation as men move through
the initiation system. I quote from Mackenzie (in press; references and
Telefol terms omitted).[53]

The feather elaborated string bag, an overt expression of sexual differentiation, is introduced at the very moment when children are first made aware of opposition between the sexes, at the beginning of the initiation cycle when a boy's masculinity is forcefully imposed . . . [54]

When adult men achieve the final level of initiation they carry the cassowary feather [string bag]. The cassowary is [a] species in which the male bird takes responsibility for the incubation of the eggs, but more significantly, in Telefol myth the cassowary is identified with Afek, the Primal Mother. When Telefol elders attach the plumes of the cassowary to the principal form, already a uterine symbol, they are creating a portable embodiment of Afek's womb, making an explicit reference to her extraordinarily potent powers.

In the context of first stage initiation, she observes, men turn themselves into male mothers in 'incubating' the boy initiates.

[And] men, as they progress through the cult, are made more aware of the importance of woman's contribution and sexual interdependence. As men grow older and less able as warriors, the emphasis shifts towards a reduction of sexual opposition. This is reflected in the cassowary feather string bag carried by male elders. The plumes on the cassowary string bag with their 'tail' referred to as 'woman's grass skirts' are suggestive of woman's appearance.

The transformations of the initiatory sequence are by necessity interior points of growth concealed from others. Only ritual specialists of the appropriate moiety affiliation will decorate the bags correctly, and at the appointed time. Mackenzie contrasts men's and women's bags to make an observation about open and secret knowledge.

The open and flexible quality of the looping of women's bags which expands readily to reveal the contents of women's bags to public scrutiny . . . reflects the open unrestricted contexts in which women loop and use bags. In this realm knowledge is openly given to those keen to know. By contrast, the feathers added by the men close over the open continuous meshwork of the female product, creating a private container in which men's secret ritual contents can be concealed. These private containers reflect

> the secluded context in which the plumage is attached,
> behind the concealing walls of the men's house . . .
> [mirroring] the way ritual knowledge is held to be secret
> and controlled.

But while the process of male growth is secret, the results are open and the stage of initiatory sequence visibly advertised in men's apparel. Each man thus presents on his exterior the effect of the secret interior process by which he has grown. What is true of individuals could also be said of communities, if we regard women and their products as 'grown' by men.

As well as men's bags, women's domestic bags also signify variation, not in their case the variation of an internal initiation hierarchy but as an external orientation towards other groups. At least from the point of view of contemporary Telefol, we know from Mackenzie's account that women both acknowledge an affinity with other Mountain Ok women — they say they make 'one kind' of bag — and "use their technical expertise to elaborate distinctive stylistic features . . . and so exaggerate the uniqueness of their product" (1986:143). People's conscious elaboration of technique creates a recognizable basic style that distinguishes the Telefol looped bag from those of other Min groups, though only certain married women master the full repertoire, and earn the right to make looped artefacts for male rituals. Both the overall shape and the texture of looping differentiate linguistic communities within the region. Mackenzie identifies at least twelve different styles of constructing the mouth opening by which, as she says, women articulate their ethnic differences.

Finally, I end with two pieces of information both indicative of the way bags do and do not travel between communities, and of the different reactions of people to letting them. The situation looks quite different from a Telefol perspective and from that of certain other Min or Ok groups.

> Recently, the opening up of the region with airstrips has increased mobility for women, and there is an accelerated diffusion of bilum styles, which is leading to a blurring in the indication of tribal distinctions. Some groups seem to be more receptive and eclectic of other's creativity. It is interesting to note that Telefol women do not exhibit any urge to copy or assimilate style elements from other Min groups — for they believe that their style is unquestionably the best. Other groups seem to agree with them, for the Telefol style is the dominant one, and has spread outwards in all directions (1986:147, references omitted):

At the same time:
> there is a resistance in Telefomin to developing the string

bag as a commodity. Telefol women display a singular lack of interest in providing bilums for an external market.[55]

The DPI marketing manager, had, in March 1984, been trying for over a year to develop a commercial bilum marketing project in Telefomin **like the highly successful project in Oksapmin** . . . where women are exporting bilums throughout PNG and overseas . . Yet all his attempts were 'totally ineffective' (Stephen Blake, pers. comm.) . . . The minimal success Blake had was when he patrolled villages personally to buy. He noted that it was those women he bought bags from who took care of him on his subsequent village rounds. Those women explained to me that they had 'seen his face and felt sorry for him.' For the Telefol women do not like to give a bilum unless they have 'seen the face of the recipient' while they are looping, and they can invest their labour in a social return (1986:164, my emphasis).

Among themselves, bags were passed along local kinship networks. In fact, the bags given away were always intended for — elicited by — specific social others (a father, a younger brother), and it is thought that the gift of a bag helps the recipient recall an image of its maker.[56] The form her activity takes is not to be elicited anonymously.

P.2. S O C I E T I E S

P.1. HISTORICAL CRITIQUE

P.1. HISTORY

P.1. Trade and Transmission. By any Western sense of history, one background to regional comparisons lies in the implicit knowledge that societies such as those found in interior Papua New Guinea are historically related. Not only do they derive from original ('genetic') material but their relative isolation was in any case always modified by the way persons and things travel. They share origins of a kind, a common history in the movement of populations, and share ideas and artefacts that travel with or without people, so they are in that sense in communication with one another.

In recent times language has been only a partial barrier to trade and only a partial barrier to the spread of information about events. Thus Barth describes how throughout the Mountain Ok area at big initiations and rituals one might expect to see delegates of senior ritual experts, and even novices, from distant groups, so that "a network of participation connects all centres and all major events throughout the area" (1987:8). There is ample evidence both of prehistoric trade and of the recent adoption of styles by people thereby in 'historical' contact with on another. The Chambri who borrowed the presence of tourists for their rituals of growth "explicitly regard their society as based on borrowing" (Errington and Gewertz 1986:99). As we have seen, not only may one linguistic population or society adopt the distinctive features of another, they may turn them into distinctive features for themselves — as happened in the 1950s and 1960s with the widespread popularity in certain Hagen areas of a wig style they referred to as distinctively 'Enga'. The example of the capping, encasing wig is apt. In Hagen, new points of growth within a clan were commonly designated by the foreign origins of incoming wives, usually other Hagen clans. it caused a momentary confusion at an early point in fieldwork to be standing on a ridge that overlooked the Baiyer valley and the mountains of Enga country in the distance, and to be told that one of the clans of the local Hagen tribe was named 'Enga-people'.

There was nothing, of course, 'Enga' about these people bar the name they carried. Nonetheless, Feil (1987:265ff) points out that the major ceremonial exchange institutions of the Enga and Hagen as well as Mendi populations in fact link some 200,000 people into a system whose different elements appear to have been transferred from one node to another and where in any case the flow of shell and pig valuables affected border relations. He speculates that Enga exchange practice 'grew from' a Hagen one in the past, or, 'was brought by Mount Hagen immigrants' to what is now Enga, first in the form of private compensation payments and then with increased production opportunities expanding into its present complex form.

So one feels that **if only one knew** in detail the actual history of actual contacts between populations, one would be able to plot and track the movement of ideas and artefacts across the region, document their variations along the way and, in lieu of the cultural analogies I have been suggesting, substitute social connections. There would be nothing unexceptional at all about the fact that particular items turn up in different contexts and with varying degrees of importance attached to them — we would provide a scale for ourselves by considering our subject matter societies in historical contact with one another.

The actualism is attractive, and anthropologists have begun documenting historical change for periods that are known about and for which we do have records, especially the history of European contact itself. As a consequence, where European contact has been longer, the historical record appears to have greater depth. That illusion has itself come under criticism for ignoring the historicity of Melanesian societies (see, for example, the essays in Gewertz and Schieffelin 1985).

Yet the facility with which Europeans traversed the landscape, the early foot patrols leaving red cloth here, steel axes there, offers a plausible kind of figure or image of pre-contact colonizers. People scattered by warfare or propelled by trade or intermarriage must have similarly traversed the Highlands interior, not the same person of course, but as individuals or groups of people travelling here, settling there, a magnification of the movement that occurred in any case as they followed paths to new gardens and shifted the location of their houses. This being the case, the question of 'connections' between different societies ceases to be a problem. What instead becomes of interest are the reasons for particular local adaptations, different trajectories of development in styles of leadership or types of transactions or whatever. Set into a social context like this, the cultural similarities across social boundaries become trivial.

In other words, the paradoxical sense is that "if only one knew" one could fill in the historical details of how things (artefacts, ideas, forms of cultural life) were transmitted between different populations, but one would not in fact be adding substantially to the knowledge of social process. The nature of communication is already known to anthropologists: people compare, borrow, adapt, turn artefacts into items for their own use. To compile a thousand instances of individual cases would give us more information about the historical relatedness of specific populations, but would not otherwise be adding to the fact that we 'know' populations are historically related. To repeat the point, the new question instead becomes the process by which local social forms developed.

When we try to pin down moments of communication, however, the absence of information can be quite daunting. We may also encounter other disconcerting phenomena. For instance, Barth notes that visiting delegates at one another's rituals may come away in a state of shock at what they have seen, and Gardner (1983:357) retells the story of an attempt between Telefolmin and Mianmin to coordinate a ritual cycle that ended in their cutting off relations. It concerns a stage in the initiation sequence, important to many Ok peoples, when potent pandanus wigs are made for the initiands. The story goes that Mianmin no longer had the knowledge for this stage and relied on Telefol elders; instead of turning up when they should, however, to the profound disgust of the elders they were distracted on the way by wild pig that they successfully hunted and ate. The lax, ignorant Mianmin were initiated by Telefolmin no more. But the story is a Mianmin one, and is of course about misplaced priorities on both sides.[57] More than that, it shows that the Mianmin already openly had what the Telefolmin were elaborately seeking by secret means — namely the kind of masculinity and potency that was revealed in hunting prowess. They had anticipated the effects of the arduous ritual. Perhaps a pragmatic effect of mutual distancing of this kind would be to reinforce local practices, enhance local uniqueness, and thus encourage adherence to local forms.

P.2. Losing Information. From another perspective, this all seems quite unremarkable. It is an ethnic convention for people self-conscious of the styles of others to enhance their own marks of distinctiveness at the same time as they are open to foreign 'influence' — to borrow this or that but turn it to their own use. Or, in the absence of specific knowledge about other ethnic congeries, one can still imagine people working on and elaborating imported forms, even though they do not know their provenance. Their internally motivated distinctions scales the anthropologist's ethnic model. Internal differentiation presents itself, for instance, in the necessity for initiation paraphernalia to indicate the relative positioning of male cult participants. It is easy to see such distinctive marks as category-creating classifiers, again an unremarkable human product. As for the materials they use, we are back to bricolage — people work with what is to hand. But what do they imagine is to hand?

"If only one knew" is a cry that, if we are to believe Barth, Baktaman elders, and their neighbors across Mountain Ok, also set up. They struggle perpetually against a sense of loss — including a sense of future knowledge loss. Barth claims that the extreme experience of entropy that Dan Jorgensen has described so poignantly for Telfolmin (e.g. 1985) cannot be generalized to Baktaman (he produces a typology of three existential moments in the way the Telefol, Baktaman and Bimin-Kuskusmin recover the past for themselves (1987:49-50)). Nevertheless, like other Faiwol speakers, Baktaman seem to live with the constant fear that vital knowledge might be lost in the future.

> With the necessity, as they see it, of deception of the
> uninitiated, and the sacralizing power of secrecy . . .
> transmission from elder to junior is in perpetual danger

of being lost: 'This was all our ancestors told us.' In cases of recognized failure of transmission, however, **the traditions of neighbouring groups are**, under fortunate circumstances, **available to replace the parts of one's own tradition that were lost** (1987:27, references omitted; my emphasis).

From witnessing a surviving ritual expert struggling to re-form in his mind an initiation sequence he had once performed and had to perform again, Barth reflects on the generation of knowledge itself. Those who would transmit knowledge to others must under these conditions first create it for themselves. He turns this insight into an elucidation of cultural variation in Mountain Ok cosmology.

Had the problem been variation in descent group structure or possibly even political organization, Barth might have been able to endorse some 'primary social fact' about groups as a starting point for analysis; however, clan structures appear as a derivative of cult performances, not the other way round. He also finds that he cannot explicate the quite radically disparate interpretations and usages which these peoples hold through models of co-variation; systematic comparisons yield little insight. Indeed, general knowledge of the workings of their own society is of little help even to the experts reconstructing a ritual sequence. And he sees no profit in an autonomous view of covariation which supposes that concepts have an internal capacity to generate opposites, inversions and the like; Barth prefers to conserve the scale on which Mountain Ok peoples apparently conduct their affairs, and does not look for a solution by modelling different levels of meanings. He thus draws on his own earlier analysis of Baktaman cosmology cast in an analogic mode. Semantic transformations are the outcome of the way specific metaphors are elaborated, leading people's interpretations in different directions. There is no single body of knowledge any more than there is a single Ok culture, but a number of small local centers.

By understanding the social mechanisms by which knowledge is made articulate, he argues, we shall better understand how it changes and varies, between generations and between local centers. The reproduction of knowledge involves constant reformulation through a dual process of subjectification and externalization. What is transmitted is not the kind of abstract systemics which Western scholars see as summative of their endeavors but the specific meaning that specific imagery has for particular experts. However, Barth seems to accept Jack Goody's observation (in the Foreword) that silent knowledge is lost knowledge, and its implied sequel, that lost knowledge is no knowledge. So the account is motivated by an attempt to understand how the Ok manage to achieve a sense of completeness in a world where they are constantly aware that transmission is a hazard, that when paraphernalia is lost or an old man dies they are robbed of a capacity to act.

Barth makes it clear that experts are concerned with providing the vehicles for thought, for making hidden meanings appear, constantly generating for themselves the very traditions that must change in the course of regeneration. Yet this must surely cancel any lingering anthropological notion that 'tradition' only survives if it is kept intact as a positive tracery of connections between events, images, meanings. We have to, as he stresses, get our ontology right. On this evidence, that exercise must surely include loss of knowledge as part of the data, not as loss of the data. If creating doubts about a distinction (as in the case of gender, where elongation of initiates' hair with pandanus leaves is also an encasing of it) forces people to new conclusions, perhaps 'losing' the conclusions of their predecessors is a further edge that the ritual experts hold.

I prefer to think of Barth's generative model as making explicit the procreativity of absence and loss that Ok people articulate when they think about their own practices — the legacy is the 'knowledge' that each generation is created out of what has been lost in previous ones.[58] Let me recast this in an imaginary scenario.

Suppose that, as some items get dropped from a repertoire, others fill their place. What fills such a gap must be items that already exist: in the place of 'two', a remaining 'one' doubles in significance (or vice versa). New variations are impressed upon each part. A possible example is to hand. The Bolovip neighbors of Baktaman cherish a multiplicity of ancestral skulls divided into two distinct sets, the one set painted red, the other white; no skull should be painted in both colors. However, the two Baktaman temples, while containing multiple ancestral relics, hold only one skull, which may be painted red, white or both colors, depending on the occasion (1987:3). In such a case — from either the Bolovip or Baktaman perspective — the necessity to keep these proportions would not be given in advance. What is presumably given in advance is the total figuration, the possibility of seeing the ancestral skull as either red or white.[59] The proportional distribution of these properties comes from having to make specific forms yield the desired images. Were this necessity projected into the past, we could recover Barth's observation that the ritual experts see their task as retrieving the imagery that will communicate their ideas and thus transform novices into 'knowing and seeing men.'

Although I refer to knowledge loss in keeping with Barth's own account, in fact information loss would be closer to the point — loss of a "degree of (semiotic) freedom . . . to choose among the available signals, symbols, messages, or patterns to be transmitted" (Wilden 1972:233).[60] It is freedom of choice that appears reduced, a reduction in specificity of form. What is lost are imagined as once existing vehicles or media for communication. But I have suggested the **knowledge** that they are lost is not, so to speak, lost knowledge, it is knowledge about absence, about forgetting and about an unrecoverable background. That sense of loss stimulates the Baktaman initiators, it would seem, to making present images work — not to filling in the gaps, for that cannot be done, but making what is present do all the differentiating work it has to do, and thus creating information for themselves. They literally have to make what is to hand. That includes borrowing from the knowledge of their neighbors. It also includes seeing an unrecoverable background in the present artefacts, for there are only these artefacts to contain it. What they yield is 'new' information.

The ritual experts, we might surmise, have to read sufficient meaning into what they perceive they are left with, in a sense to force what they now hold to carry the marks of a lost complexity. Thus they may create internal differentiations in lieu of what they think were once two separate ritual stages.[61] Perhaps seeing their own activities, like so many particles of dust, against a huge background of ignorance is what spurs their efforts. This ignorance is not of the unknowable: it is of what has been dropped from the repertoire, the intervening particles that once completed what is now left. In order to retain a sense of multiplicity and proportional enlargement, they must break the remaining 'small' unit down into 'smaller' units. At the same time, communication between senior experts from different communities means they always have the choice to supplement their repertoire from elsewhere. The important thing is that the gaps are preserved. They do not see themselves as recreating what they think is missing, but only what they know. It is as if they knew that by insisting on that absence they create their own creativity.

If so, this adds a footnote to the concept of prefiguration. In one sense, everything is in place: sociality, the values, relationships. But what must be constantly made and remade, invented afresh, are the forms in which such things are to appear. Potency has to appear as a new-born child or a bursting yam house, or a successful hunt, strength as shouldering a tall spirit-effigy, in the same way as social persons have to appear as members of this or that group. So those Melanesians who have origin stories, speak of heroes scattering the land **with the right form** in which tools or food or sexual attributes or named groups should appear, just as the Gawan ancestress did. She did not have to show the men how to make a canoe — that they knew — but in showing them the appropriate materials, she showed them the appropriate form it should take.

The sense of lost forms that afflicts some of the Mountain Ok people means that they do indeed have to make the form they hold yield the totality of society. In the absence of 'multiple' further possibilities, the 'one' form, the one initiation sequence or whatever, must do multiple work.

P.2.   EVOLUTION

<u>P.1.   Leaders into the Future</u>.   It was the prominent interpreter role of Baktaman elders that led Barth to ponder on their part in transforming the cultural repertoire. Through control of knowledge, and through personal responsibility to recreate certain forms, some individuals exert a disproportionate influence over what gets transmitted. Rather similar figures dominate another comparative exercise published in the same year, Feil's discussion of the evolution of Highlands societies.

Here are men with the future on their backs. For his complex account of the kinds of developments in pig husbandry and horticultural techniques that encouraged the diversification of social forms in prehistorical and historical times is fuelled by the energies of those seeking to enhance or enlarge their sphere of influence through wealth exchanges. These figures are big men and their prototypes, those who in extending power over persons also hold the power to shape the development of society. With such entrepreneurial spirits, one does not have to linger over the question of how traditional forms are transmitted.

A prefiguring of a sorts provides a background to Feil's analysis, namely the assumption that social mechanisms for evolution are already in place. Indeed, merely to change analytical perspective from thinking about culture to thinking about society provides such a background. Two such mechanisms are implied in the very notion of social organization.

One is that of internal differentiation: in this view, it is important to know the distribution of power within societies. These are not homogeneous cultures. On the contrary, every society is composed of distinct interest groups, and social analysis is essential to tell one who in fact controls 'the culture' — hence the observer sustains a dual interest in ideology on the one hand and in relations of production on the other. The supposition about interest groups becomes a spur to the anthropologist to disentangle the conduct of social relations, and the structure of control over production and distribution, from the smokescreen (Josephides 1983) of ideology. Second, and related to this view, is the expectation of appropriation. Here, an impetus to social complexification lies in the appropriation by some persons of what belongs to or is distinctive about others.   The Mendi apparently regard the pig festival that is their most important expression of clan solidarity as only recently adopted (Lederman 1986:21). Internally, appropriation may mean directing the actions of certain others, and most typically anthropologists have looked at the way men exploit women's labors. This appropriation constitutes specific relations of production and inequalities among men and between men and women. The way in which Melanesians conceive of themselves as being creative through containing *the growing points of others* can thus be turned into a causal explanation on the anthropologist's part for differing forms of social organization.

Feil's own comparative concern is the evident ecological and economic contrast between societies in the Eastern and in the Western Highlands. He sees it as a result of the divergent development of two distinct economic formations (1987:9). The material facts he assembles are impressive. One might be a little puzzled, then, that one of his dramatic cross-societal contrasts, the respective scattering and centering of huge populations, could almost reflect the tiny transhumant movements that a few hundred Umeda make between their sojourn in bush gardens and their coming together for major festivals in ridge-top villages.[62] Werbner (1989:189) emphasizes the fact that phases of this annual Umeda cycle are marked by different forms of social organization. However, there is also a major orientation to Feil's study, for his is not a relative view. Rather, he offers a particular perspective from those institutions which demonstrate the culmination of societal development, *viz.* the 'complex' exchange systems of Enga and Hagen.

He argues that the area around Mount Hagen is the probable 'birth-place' of intensive agriculture in the Highlands and that "the development of these two [Enga and Hagen] exchange systems is the direct outgrowth of that earliest, intensive horticultural regime, [and the] related pig production which depended upon it" (1987:263). For him, Hagen is the original growing point, agricultural and pig surpluses there accompanying an expanding population, though the Enga version of the exchange system is at the pinnacle of organizational complexity. Across the spectrum of Highlands societies, as he puts it (1987:268), "only some have developed exchange institutions" on this scale. Elsewhere people remain divided by parochial issues and live out small-scale lives. He argues that intensification goes hand in hand with an economic rationality which lodges, if nowhere else, in the ambitions of big men. It is of some satisfaction for his account that as one moves westwards towards Hagen and Enga, the initiation of boys becomes secondary to the promotion of pig festivals, foreshadowing the increasing significance of domestic pig festivals. This shift he correlates with others. Whereas in the Eastern Highlands flutes by legend stolen from women were also used to terrorize them, where they occur in the west they are simply regarded as male inventions. He suggest that it is "precisely at this point in the continuum of highlands societies that. . . the flute complex as a symbol of male hegemony collapses and male initiations as mystifications of male superiority cease" (1987:213). For here women become openly recognized as "crucial participants in their societies' vital exchange systems."

In countering possible objections to his rather sanguine portrait of female participants, he suggests that the most antagonistic and exploita-tive male-female relations occur in societies where intensive pig husbandry and horticulture are recent. In the mature societies of the Western Highlands by contrast, where such intensive production is much older, women developed 'high status' from a dual role in pig production and kinship networks. Exchange relations became a focus of undivided attention, and the orientation of production was itself thereby transformed (1987:231-2).

Feil thus envisages a gradient of increasing social complexity, including (among many factors), a gradient from a hegemonic dichotomy between the sexes to the 'hierarchical' and 'complex' system of Hagen, for which he resurrects an older class vocabulary.[63] His argument is that marked ecological and cultural differences across the Highlands above all indicate that these societies have had different histories. The result is seen in the varying configurations (e.g. 1987:5) they present. If the problem is to make sense a mass of detail, the solution is that such configurations can be given both a historical placement (in terms of increasing complexity) and a geographical one (on an east-west continuum). Feil's spatial-temporal perspective is intended to provide an evolutionary trajectory as the crucial coordinating scale, and thus yield a rank order, for apprehending variations between contemporary societies.

P.2. The Elaboration of Relationships. It is facile to criticize work as wideranging as Feil's by introducing overlooked complexities from other perspectives. Nonetheless, there is a most provocative 'remainder' to his exercise, both one of its crucial dimensions and one that exceeds the task he has set himself. This is entailed in the concept of complexity itself.

Feil deploys the concept strictly in relation to agricultural intensification and the elaboration of exchange relationships. I make my point through an exaggeration. Perhaps one can imagine whole societies or systems as more or less complex along certain specific dimensions, such as division of labor or technological specialism. But if one takes social relationships in general as the elements out of which Westerners abstract their notion of society, then I do not know by what criteria of involution, feedback, levels of internal organization, or intricate structure one would decide that relations in one Highlands society were more complex than those in another.

Social relations are a phenomenon an outsider cannot describe without participating in indigenous formulations. In her critique of the kind of historical understanding anthropologists and others have brought to Papua New Guinea societies, Lederman (1986:20) suggests that the indigenous analog to the Western historian's 'event' lies in recognized nodes of social relationship: "the achievement of relationship is what shapes a happening into a meaningful category of experience." Thus what is preserved in the names of persons Mendi recall on this or that occasion becomes the memory of social alignments and their significance for the future, the realization of or anticipated 'appearance' of relations. It follows that the present does not repeat the past so much as make it appear; in which case the present is already in place as a version of the past. So might we imagine complexity 'already' there, in the recursive imagery of sociality.

Let us go back to the humble string bag from Telefol, beyond the central Highlands and a low production society by Feil's criteria. Appropriated or not by men depending on one's perspective, Telefol string bags are hardly anonymous products with a value only for exchange purposes: they do not exist apart from the relationships out of which they are made and for which they either bear women's produce or men's personal paraphernalia. In fact, their manufacture is elicited by known others. In the same way as specific forms appear through the juxtapositioning of figures in a masquerade, the acts of specific persons are elicited by the social acts of others. In the domestic context in which bags circulate, relationships are always particular, persons so to speak always known, and thus 'carried' (Wagner in press) by others.

Perhaps I am influence by the dominant form of gift exchange in Hagen, the *moka* gesture of 'more', where an addition tops a return. But I would understand elicitation itself as an act of elaboration or exaggeration. This is so for the most routine and minute behaviors, as well as for grand gestures. The form an act takes — the growing of boys or the satisfaction of a maternal brother or a gift to a sibling — acquires a specific substance and materiality in its being made present. This presence is 'more' than the obligation or protocol, the social norm, which demanded it in the first place. The man who begs a bag from his sister finds that he also carries on his back a permanent memorial of her features.

It is hardly surprising, then, that we should encounter not just individuals enhancing and enlarging their own spheres of influence under favorable demographic or economic circumstances, but widespread interest in the elaboration of relationships as such. The enactment or realization of a relationship is an elaboration on its existence. In making connections visible, people assert their ever-present capacity to act upon them. At least, this is one way to read Paula Rubel and Abraham Rosman's (1978) excursus through a dozen societies throughout Papua New Guinea, and through relationships based on cult association, kinship ties, moiety opposition, ritual sponsorship, political aggression, warfare, ceremonial exchange, intermarriage and so forth. Whether through the singing of songs, the killing of pigs or interdictions on sexual relations, everywhere relations are made evident in highly elaborated form.

Rubel and Rosman suggest a sequence of transformations across societies in terms of the apparent evolution of particular relationships. In some societies, for instance, the relationship between affines carries the burden of initiatory duties or the structure of ceremonial exchange, while elsewhere its significance is diminished and ritual experts or specialist exchange partners overshadow the affinal tie. A relationship important in one society thus appears reduced or insignificant in another. In analyzing these variations as transformations, they propose a common scale of development, with branches going off in this or that direction. The relative development of affinal relations and exchange partnerships is taken as diagnostic (e.g. Rubel and Rosman 1978:333). Transformations operate both within and between societies. For example, two different structures of exchange, transforms of each other, may occur in the one society. Comparisons between the exchange structures of different societies in addition enable them to set up a prototype, and characterize certain contemporary societies as nearer to, others divergent from ('independent transformations of'), the prototype. Hagen and Enga again fall at one end of a series. However, the concept of relative degrees of elaboration rests on *a priori* judgement about what relationship one actually sees.

By what prior knowledge do we in fact decide we are looking at the actions of affines on this occasion, of exchange partners on that? If the prototype for an exchange partner is an affine, then why do we not classify all exchange partners as 'affines' — some being affines with women trafficked between them, and some being affines with masks or shells trafficked between them? If Western systematics insists on an overarching term that would signal their combined dissimilarity and similarity, then we could classify both sets of persons as 'exchange partners', divided into affines and allies (Umeda), or classify both sets as 'allies', divided into affines and exchange partners (Hagen)!

We have, in fact, arrived at the same impasse of form reached earlier in considering artefacts. To that extent, the solution is already prefigured: what should hold our attention are the analogies people draw between the various relationships which constitute sociality for them. Anthropological typologizing already draws on indigenous analogies but does so partially, for it ignores their scaling. Perhaps one could complete the move like this.

An affine is one of the forms in which an exchange partner in Hagen may appear, as an exchange partner is one of the forms in which an affine can appear. Neither is isomorphic with the other, neither a subtype. Rather, each is a version of the other. But the one relationship seen from the perspective of the other, as we might imagine affines embarking on a *moka* sequence as exchange partners, is an elaboration or augmentation on the relationship. This does not necessarily mean the elaboration is added at will. On the contrary, elaboration may be according to protocol. An affine may fail his in-law if he does not become an exchange partner: yet when he does, he does not just realize the affinity between them, he adds to the that affinity by his conduct as a partner. This also works in reverse, as when potential exchange partners seek to consolidate their transactions through intermarriage. They add another dimension to their relationship. In coming into existence, the new dimension both realizes the pre-existing relationship and in giving it a specific (material, substantial) form encapsulates the prior relationship in a new one. Relationships are made up of the constant recapitulation of prior ones (Gillison in press).

In the same way as a bridewealth prestation is both a displacement of and a transformation of betrothal payments, or a child both contains and anticipates parenthood — so every relationship people make appears in this sense a development or version of others. The difference between affines and exchange partners is like the difference between a boy and a man or between a woman with a full and with an empty string bag down her back. Yet the imagery of the bag misleads if it suggests that there is some prototype beyond which all is elaboration: on the contrary, the empty bag is as 'full' of significance as the one heavy with produce. Relationships always appear in the signifying dimension of enlargement, for that is how they are made to appear, taking specific form and presence from the enactment of people's intentions and obligations.

No wonder it is hard to pin down what is of central significance in these societies, to sort out what is important and unimportant without adjudication shifting from one perspective to another. No wonder it is difficult to explain relationships by relationships, so that when anthropologists look across Highlands societies what puzzles them is the emphasis given now to this and now to that. No wonder it is even difficult sometimes to decide what is present and absent (Barth 1987:20). Social relationships are complex by definition: they exist as outgrowths from one another. Perhaps the same should be said of the societies themselves.

It is nice thought, except that one is not able to specify the mechanism of elicitation. Moreover, while the Papua New Guineans in question, and other Melanesians probably as well, might have a concept of growth and outgrowth, they do not have a concept of society in the indigenous Western sense. So we are back to the same mix of metaphors that characterized some of the anthropological positions presented earlier.

P.2. PROSTHETIC EXTENSIONS

P.1. ADDITIVES

P.1. Partial Explanations. Contemplating the difficulties of describing, across the spectrum of Papua New Guinean societies, even the reasonably-well delimited phenomenon of male initiation led Keesing (1982) to refer to a multidimensional understanding and to what he dubs Bateson's problem. The problem in Gregory Bateson's exegesis of the Iatmul *naven* was not how to fit together different parts of Iatmul society but how to fit together in his account different sources of anthropological explanation.[64] No paradigm seemed global. Keesing suggests we should recognize the attendant challenge of bridge-building between partial explanations. "'Bateson's problem' remains. If ecological, economic, sociological, political, symbolic, psychological, and other partial explanations of New Guinea men's cults and initiation rituals are to be mutually reinforcing and suppletive, rather then mutually exclusive, we need some framework in which they can be fitted together" (1982:32).

One among the explanations that Keesing considers for the transformation of New Guinea economies and sociopolitical structures, and thus to the present-day variation that comparison reveals, is intensification of root-crop production (1982:35). When Feil looks closely at the process of intensification, he finds that the causes are hard 'to sort out.' Feil himself sketches in the complexity of the problem by reference to environmental degradation, competition with neighbors, a desire for high quality protein, and so forth, and suggests that these may all be useful but remain "partial interpretations" (1987:58). Then, when Pierre Lemonnier examines horticultural regimes within closely related populations among the Anga, he finds at least three variant arrangements to the simple sequence of burning/planting/fencing gardens, and can summon only "partial explanations" for the internal patterning of technological traits (1989:160).[65] Yet we only have to pause over what is meant by explanation to realize that there are different types of explanation, of which causal connection is only one. Between different logical forms any fit is bound to appear partial. This brings us back to one of the positions from which this present account started, the sufficiency of representation where representation subsumes explanation. In John Peel's 1987 paper on History, Culture and the Comparative Method, explanation subsumes comparison (see footnote 5).

Between these theoretical positions, we move from needing to find explanations for our facility to make comparisons to finding comparison implicit in any explanation. However, this expansion and contraction of concepts is not finished yet: needless to say, Peel then produces five different types of comparative procedures. Since, as he says, we **should** distinguish them (1987:90), he must mean that usually we do not and usually proceed with a muddle of incommensurate methods.

Here is a kind of replicative process, where each configuration of concepts produces a remainder that generates a new dimension. The result is a set of strategies that the trope of perspective does not in the end sufficiently describe. The idea of there being numerous perspectives and viewpoints 'on' phenomena implies that one could ideally formulate some kind of summation of all possible views, or at least a framework or perhaps a generative model for the production of the perspectives themselves. But that would not account for the sense of movement or journey that one has in switching perspectives, nor for one's implicit knowledge that the number of possible perspectives is in fact infinite. For that number is equal to the number of things from whose vantage one could see the world, or to the number of purposes for which one might wish to see, **plus one**: plus the perspective that would result from seeing the world via perspective. No matter how many perspectives are assembled, they all create perspective. The formal product is infinity (cf. Mimica 1988:122).

The various positions through which I have led this account could look as though they form a series of perspectives. But I have tried to make them work in a particular way — to make it evident that, as a constellation of elements, each position generates a further elaboration with an enlarging and diminishing effect on the constellations of the previous position.

I have both drawn on arguments within anthropology that focus on narrative strategy, and made my narrative out of the kinds of information that provoke anthropological enquiry. The attention to comparison does not so much offer fresh prescriptions for a comparative method, as indicate one of the ways anthropologists create complexities for themselves, and thus their sense of having to get things into proportion. As a running commentary on this, I also introduced various Melanesian materials that give insight into other and different orders of complexity. Pressed thus into service, such materials are necessarily already part of the anthropological data. One can only be deliberate about comparison; hence the differences and similarities between the two principal parts of this monograph indicate Western/Melanesian (see footnote 1) parallels and indicate the artifice of the construction. Indeed, I have deliberately tried to find analogs in Melanesian experience to the academic experience that, contrary to what some of our models tell us, complexity keeps its own scale. As we sift through the contexts and levels of our materials, we find that enlarging or diminishing this or that set of problems does not seem to increase or decrease the complexity of information itself. At the same time, not all of the different pieces of information, the sets of complexities, are equal to one another; they are suspended in some kind of relativity.

So I have also tried to do something else, which is reveal the tip of an Achilles heel. That is, to reveal that despite the extreme attempt at artifice, I am not in complete control of the account, and that the phenomenon of remaindering that I have contrived also comes unbidden. The Melanesian material has been necessary to realize that.

P.2. Cut-outs and Wholes. One motive for wishing to have things fit together may lie in the prior supposition that they have been cut out of something. This is an effect which Robert Thornton locates in the writing of ethnography itself. He draws an analogy between the description of a social structure and the plot of a narrative, both exemplifying "the image of coherence and order that writing creates" (1988a:286; cf. Clifford 1988:Ch. 3). Although the closure of an ethnography is a rhetorical device that appears to complete its subject matter, he implies that the same point is applicable to other anthropological writing as well. It may be, he says, "that it is impossible to conceptualize society, except in terms of holistic images" (1988a:289) — a point immediately opened up in a footnote which reads that society as the object of sociological description must not be confused with the social, "the experience of other people and our relationship with them" (1988a:301).

Ethnography's essential fiction, Thornton argues, is that the social whole consists of parts. Many theoretical arguments are phrased in terms of part-whole relations, whether the parts are persons, institutions, symbols or whatever. He then adds a complexity: there are two types of wholes. One is properly mereological, where the same relationship holds for the whole as for the parts, as a branch is part of a tree; the other is the rule of class-inclusion by which analytical categories constitute members of a set. He suggests that in the interests of rhetorical coherence, and thus "for evoking the imagination of wholeness" (1988a:292) the two are often conflated. Images such as bodies and trees serve the conflation, good mereological metaphors imparting both naturalness and wholeness to analytical structures that in fact rest on rules of class-inclusion. Textual parts are confused with social parts.

Thus Thornton comments on the incommensurability between what are taken as segments of social totalities such as clans, age-grades, nations on the one hand, and textual segments such as chapters, title headings, paragraphs on the other. In the latter case, the parts are mereologically constitutive of a whole; in the former there is no relation of consistency between these elements or particles — they do not add up — and do not form social wholes the way the textual analogy leads us to think (1988a:291). In **either** case, however, 'parts' are created in the very idea of 'cutting' elements from an imagined and encompassing entity. Thus the rhetoric of analysis works as the decomposition of an imagined society or culture. The imagery of cutting, one might add, adds a correlative sense of unity or wholeness to the individual parts insofar as they can be considered on their own.[66]

However, these days not all texts are intended to 'add up'. Texts that do not add up are purportedly found in postmodern genres that deliberately juxtapose narrative incommensurables. The realization that wholeness is rhetoric itself is relentlessly exemplified in collage, or collections that do not collect but display the intractability of the disparate elements. Yet such techniques of showing that things do not add up paradoxically often include not less cutting but **more** — a kind of hypercutting of perceived events, moments, impressions. And if elements are presented as so many cut-outs, they are inevitably presented as parts coming from other whole cloths, larger pieces, somewhere. When the cosmopolitan is thought of as 'rootless', this is exactly the kind of cut that is made.

The contemporary metaphor of cutting derives power from further connotations of disruption. Indeed, rupture as such is thought of as destructive, iconoclastic. The trope runs throughout Clifford's **Predicament of Culture**. There he observes (1988:43; original emphasis) how

> [b]oth Crapanzano and Dwyer seek to represent the research experience in ways that tear open the textualized fabric of the other, and thus also of the interpreting self. (Here etymologies are evocative: the word **text** is related, as is well known, to weaving, **vulnerability** to rending or wounding, in this instance the opening up of a closed authority.)

He is explicit about wishing, instead of a search after some seamless vision, to apprehend the materials of ethnographic writing as "meaningful artefacts cut up, salvaged" yet in turn always susceptible to reassembly and "creative recombination" (1988:12). Creativity in this view is thus what one makes do with, the recombining of parts unkindly cut from their original loci, even though one knows that those loci must have been cut from others. His chapter on Marcel Griaule suggests that ethnographic fieldwork itself can be seen as an intrinsically violent and intrusive extraction, Griaule merely acting out, as it were, the aggressiveness of all collectors of artefacts. Thus Clifford cites a study of museum collections that shows how exhibits "create the illusion of adequate representation of a world by first cutting objects out of specific contexts (whether cultural, historical, or intersubjective) and making them 'stand for' abstract wholes" (1988:220). As he says of collage (1988:146, original emphasis), it

> brings to the work (here the ethnographic text) elements that continually proclaim their foreigness to the context of presentation. These elements — like a newspaper clipping or a feather — are marked as real, as collected rather than invented by the artist-writer. The procedures of (a) cutting out and (b) assemblage are of course basic

to any semiotic message; here they **are** the message. The
cuts and sutures of the research process are left visible;
there is no smoothing over or blending of the work's
raw data into a homogeneous representation. To write
ethnographies on the model of collage would be to avoid
the portrayal of cultures as organic wholes.

Appositely, he cites Bateson's *Naven* as an example.

There are other ways than organicism, he advocates, to imagine cultural
creativity. Or rather, his imagery of grafting hints at regeneration rather
than reproduction. Exactly as the cosmopolitan grows from no one place,
no single set of roots, so the heterogeneity of the world's cultures, creolized,
transmuted, have to generate by other means than rooting. Culture and
identity need not take root in ancestral plots, he says, but can live by
pollination and transplanting. Clifford speaks not in the poignant mood
of entropy but in a kind of nostalgic hypertrophy — there are too many
pasts to be gathered. In his account, the gathering and tying still seems
the creative act. With Melanesians in mind — with their open borrowings
and appropriations — catch the cadence of this sentence:[67]

> The roots of tradition are cut and retied, collective symbols
> appropriated from external influences (1988:13).

I have Melanesians in mind, of course, because the image of 'cutting'
can be put to quite different tropic usage, as becomes evident from the
works of Gillison (1980, in press) and J. Weiner (1987, 1988). Relations
are created in the separation of persons from one another. Where rupture
consequently carries connotations of creativity, one does not need to imagine
a kind of wholeness, or a kind of reassembled life, from tying bits together.

Take the recent discussions on the desirability of dialogue as a vehicle
for modelling cross-cultural experience that is also inter-subjective experience. A Melanesian viewpoint would add to Clifford's pertinent critique.
Clifford points out (1988:43) that if interpretive authority is based on the
exclusion of dialogue, purely dialogical authority would repress the inescapable
act of textualization. Take instead the reciprocity of exchange partners.
A Melanesian might comment that in any case there can be no exchange
of perspectives between ethnographer and informant for as long as the
ethnographer insists on sharing viewpoints. As social persons, they need
to be separated, indeed severed, before an exchange can take place, before
the analogy between their perspectives can work to creative effect, before
they are seen to be the same kinds of persons differentiated simply by
the positions they occupy.

P.2. CYBORGS

P.1. Cantor's dust. The tourists who came away confused and discomforted from their witnessing of a Chambri initiation sequence perhaps caught some of the anger of the boys whose earlier cuts had been freshly opened by the rough handling. Initiation practices deliberately intrude on what a Westerner would see as the boundary of a person — whether in constricting and encasing initiates' bodies in houses or phallocrypts or through letting blood or inducing loss of physical control. Melanesians do not metaphorically cut tradition, but may literally cut the surface of the skin. And they do not metaphorically turn a person upside down so that he or she has to journey in search of cultural roots, but may literally upend roots to show how the canopy was supported by them all the time.

The literalism should not mislead us. What is being cut and being made to move is the imagery itself. When men and trees and spirits and flutes and women and canoes can all be seen as analogs of one another, then when a tree is felled and brought into the center of a plaza, as in Wantoat, people are cutting the tree out of the forest as an image of a man, and when the man dances with the effigy above his head he makes the combined image of tree and forest move between himself and the edifice he supports. Look at what the Usen Barok of New Ireland do to forest trees.

Barok hold rituals in a stone enclosure that includes the men's house (Wagner 1986b, 1987). The whole is laid out in the image of a horizontal tree. At the entrance is a stile in the form of forked branches likened to a treetop, while at the rear of the house is the burial ground of ancestors likened to the roots of the clan or the roots of its 'branches', the localized matrilineage. When a person buried in the cemetery is finally decomposed, an open feast is held to end the period of restrictions on the men's house; pigs are displayed facing the stile and thus display the plentitude of the clan at the tips of its growing points, the upper branches of the 'trees' with (as they say) fruits for others to eat. However, at a culminating feast that consummates a collectivity of deaths occurring over a period, the entire horizontal structure is lifted vertically into the air; in shifting its axis it also becomes inverted.

The shift takes place outside the enclosure. A large forest tree is erected upside down, its roots in the air and its trunk now 'cut' by the ground where one might imagine its invisible branches to be spreading. As though hanging from these branches, nubile women of the lineage sit like so many upended fruits, taking on the role normally ascribed to men of marrying into lineages of other clans and giving them nurturance, while atop the tap root that before had been identified with the maternal ancestress of the clan stands an initiate big-man on the pigs slaughtered for the feast. In his 1987 paper, Wagner observes that this is

no simple inversion but a methodical and consistent
figure-ground reversal . . . of the meaningful imagery
of Barok life. It does not simply negate, it consummates
its denial by demonstrating also that the inversion makes
as much sense as the order it inverts — . . . that a man
can be taproot of a maternal line, that young women,
who constitute lineages, can also be seen as nurturance
bestowed elsewhere (1987:61).

Wagner's theoretical point is not just that roots and branches, ancestresses
and big-men, are seen to be versions of one another, but that the process
of movement from one axis to another makes people aware of their own
perceptual faculties in creating images. They perceive the figure-ground
reversal. Barok call this 'power', and it is the power of imagery. The reversal
constitutes "an image of transformation formed by the transformation of
an image" (1987:62). Hence, the effect is as though it were the image
alone that moves: ancestress and big-men are already there.

The perception elicited by these practices exceeds the anthropological
convention that images are open to multiple interpretations, affording
different tropes. The perception is rather that images contain other images
— the upright tree growing in the ground anticipates the inverted tree
with its roots in the air. Each presents a quite specific configuration of
elements, but each extends others in its effect. The inverted mortuary tree
becomes an outgrowth from the idea of an upright tree in the forest or
of the horizontal 'tree' of the enclosure for that matter. The turning is
literally tropic. Growth, reversal, cutting are all Melanesian metaphors for
the way in which one image displaces another. Consequently, one image
elicited from another displaces it in the same way as a body may be opened
to reveal the other bodies it contains: a bamboo bursts to show the persons
within, a boy grows into a man. An act of severance connects what is
separated: one 'cuts open' an exchange partnership to make valuables
move between donor and recipient. It is relationships that the cuts reveal,
including the relationships that people carry on their backs.

Insofar as figure-ground reversal presents ground as potential figure,
the movement implies that figures 'cut out' of the ground are not figures
added to it. But nor are they fragments, and this is not a part-whole
relationship. Rather, figure and ground work as two dimensions. They are
self-scaling — not two perspectives as it were, but a perspective seen twice,
ground as another figure, figure as another ground. Since each behaves
as an invariant in relation to the other, the dimensions are not constituted
in any totalising way. Hence the perception that quantity and life may
increase in the one dimension without increasing in the other: in the
elaboration of relationships, it is the elaborations that increase, not the
relationships.

On the face of it, the inversions of the Barok feasting tree are isomorphic. Branches and roots replicate one another in equal proportion. At the same time, the one is seen to grow out of the other, and one must be cut from the other as branches are literally lopped when the trunk is put into the ground. Of course, Barok appear to us to have chosen an apt root metaphor. The background to their choice is already there, in the necessity to celebrate the fertility of the clan with its neophyte big man and its ancestral support. It is this grounding sociality that the entire performance realizes, more embracing than the particular acts of making present this man or those young girls by upending the roots and cutting the branches. But while it embraces all acts, no amount of action adds to this dimension of sociality. As a ground to action, sociality cannot be increased as though it were an amount to be added to. The acts increase; it is they that divide and redivide like flecks of Cantor's dust.

Perhaps some of the Western anxiety attendant on the 'assembling' and 'tying' endeavors of those who despair at a world full of parts and cut-outs comes from the fact that where cutting is regarded as destructive, then the hypothetical social whole must thereby seem mutilated, fragmented. One feels for a body losing its limbs. But where cutting is done as in some of these Melanesian examples with the intent of making relationships appear, eliciting responses, being able to hold the donor's gift in one's hand, in short, where cutting is a creative act, it displays the internal capacities of persons and the external power of relationships. Thus, in these capacities or powers, sociality in turn appears to 'move' like a figure against a background of persons and relationships.

Cantor's dust suggests an allegory between how Melanesians thus handle imagery and how anthropologists handle the partial manifestation of the connections they presume must exist.

Baktaman elders can only work with what is present. In so doing they create new information, new repositories of the differences they wish to impress on others, and thereby see in the background the presumed skills of past experts whose absent artefacts cannot be recovered. Telefol women like to see the face of the recipient of their string bags as they do the looping. The bag does not only evoke the person, so (after Battaglia) does the empty space it encloses. For in her thoughts the woman anticipates the personal objects that the man will place there, and what is held by the string loops is not the loops themselves. Or one might think of the Wantoat decorations that bemused Schmitz.

I briefly mentioned certain hourglass-drum designs (see Figure 1). The row of drums seemed obvious shapes to Schmitz, once he knew they were called drums. His description (1963:94) makes it clear, however, that his first perception was of the intervening gaps that were painted white. And indeed these too have a name, the term for belly or the inside of a body. But with their pinched rhomboid effect, they did not really look like anything at all; he treats the drum name as significant, and the belly name as insignificant infill.[68] The fact that immediately below it is another band that depicts a row of vertebrae does not modify his priorities. Indeed, he observes of one row of ornamentation that it **only serves to fill the space**.

Yet if one releases oneself from such priorities, one can let the eye move between the sounding drums and the hollow bodies, each background for the other. Drumplaying gives life to people's bodily performances, even as they have no life of their own except as extensions of the bodies of people. Wantoat elaborate on the mobility of their figures. It is what animates them.

> All these movable ornaments, whatever their shape, were called *kong-ep* in the Wantoat valley. *Kong* is the general name for spirit, and *-ep* is really the affix denoting the locative. Thus *kong-ep* should be translated as in the spirit or on the spirit . . . As the movability of the dancing-ornaments was not restricted to particular forms, it must be meant to indicate a characteristic common to all spirits. Round and oval bark-boards bearing the 'face-design' were also made to slide up and down on bamboo poles (Schmitz 1963:120).

The mobility is effected by the supporting edifice — yet however much the moving images seem to extend into space, they do not extend the scaffolding that supports them or the forest from which the materials were cut.

Cantor's dust caught my imagination as a set of instructions for creating gaps between events by increasing the perception of a background that does not itself increase. But it is, of course, an ungainly cyborg of a thought, for it does not quite do as a complete analogy for what I am trying to describe in Melanesia, except that what I am trying to describe there is evoked by the problems of proportion in anthropological writing itself. It is a cyborg of a thought because applied to non-mathematical phenomena it has the effect of showing how we mix our metaphors. Yet anthropologists are always mixing metaphors out of 'our' and 'their' experiences, as I did in imagining connections between societies as a series of outgrowths. Suppose, then, the mix creates a circuit of disparate dimensions. One might imagine that outgrowth as a movement against a dimension that itself does not grow.

Gaps seem to give us somewhere to extend: space for our prosthetic devices. Absent expertise, the features of a distant kinsman, a glimpsed spirit elicit their imagining while also eliciting the perception that all images are borrowed images. A sense of excess or insufficiency, then, of lack of proportion, of connections being partial suggest we could extend the perceptions themselves.

P.2.   Writing Anthropology. When Usen Barok wish to put on one of their feasts, they follow strict protocol. But its form is not realized in rules or a plan: men describe a feast through narrating events as they occured, through imagining that it was taking place as they talked. The very order and sequence of such an occasion is pieced together from remembered other occasions (Wagner n.d.). Conversely, recalling its form moves them to act, its significance the one thing on which people agree. However, they do not require one another's (verbal) interpretations to sustain this communication: indeed, individual interpretations in the eyes of these New Ireland skeptics are likely to get in the way.

In somewhat similar vein, the people of Elmdon in the Essex of the 1960s were all agreed that Elmdon was a village — even as to the values to be put on staying there or going away. But that did not imply that they shared common interpretations (cf. Cohen 1986; Rapport 1986). On the contrary, it was very apparent that although half the village thought Elmdon was a community the other half were equally clear that it was not. While everyone talked about 'real villagers' and 'newcomers', no two adjudications were completely the same, and the effectiveness of the image did not depend on that. I might also return to the presentation of feminist pluralism. Having identified certain themes common to feminist enquiry, Lizbeth Stanley and Sue Wise note that "all feminists share the belief that these themes are important; [but] what we dispute is the exact meaning and implication of these for theory, for research, and for how we live our everyday lives" (1983:51). Beyond their "basic acceptance . . . there is little which is commonly accepted and shared among feminists . . . We interpret their meanings [of these themes] according to our own situations and understandings;" ongoing debate is precisely about, as they say, "what these themes **mean**, and what consequences they have for action" (1985:55, transposed; original emphasis). The perception that individual interpretations are partial imparts a background significance to the debate itself.

Care over what a feast looks like, agreement as to how real a villager is, or disputes as to what feminism does, lead to interactions evoked by what is sensed as given. The background is already there. Reworking these concerns does not simply produce a series of versions or variations. In the way that a tool extends the user's capability, reuse is also a fresh realization of the given capacity to use the tool at all, as we speak of culture as forever being invented. For a person, such imaginings are enablements, like prosthetic extensions. The person is not merely drawn into another context, the spectator or consumer of other worlds, but is made able to act. At least, that is what Barth implies when he describes the efforts of a Baktaman elder to plan a particular sequence. A previous performance of the ritual had first to be reconstructed in his mind. The elder and his colleagues saw their task as one of recall, with (Barth notes) subsidiary questions arising of whether they should copy the rites of a neighboring community or adopt new procedures for certain parts (1987:26). The (pre-existing) form had to be made present in order for them to take action.[69] The ritual was regenerated, not reproduced.

*   *   *   *   *   *

I would make a difference out of these examples. Villagers define being a real Elmdoner according to who has travelled between places or who has stayed in one place. In this English view, persons acquire identity from the places they are at, modified by where they have come from and where they are going. Places stay, persons move, and a further cultural slip is made from geographical to class location. Classes are fixed, individuals mobile. In the same way, feminist interlocutors occupy different metaphorical places. To change theoretical positions is to change political or academic character. Moving between locations can thus seem an act of disorientation. Indeed, Western geography combines with a perception of individual mobility to partition the sense of place. "This century," writes Clifford (1988:13) "has seen a drastic expansion of mobility, including tourism, migrant labor, immigration, urban sprawl." The result is felt to be fragmented persons and cultures: exoticism in an adjoining neighborhood, familiarity at the other ends of the earth. This contemporary Western sense of fragmented identity is intimately bound up with the doubly disorienting effects of travelling between places and the discovery that travel then makes places change their character. Yet the Melanesians I have been referring to are, culturally speaking, already there. They make the places travel.

If a person's identity is located in a shell valuable or encased in a bag or at the growing tips of a tree, it is these — the valuables, the bags, the trees — that travel out of sight, are put on and taken off, are turned upside down. A pearl shell is a place, we might say, that walks between persons. All these things pass between people, decorate them and support them. The centers of others become centers for oneself. Insofar as 'places' can appear now in one person and now in another, then it is the places that seem mobile. At least, Melanesians use locational devices to make this fact itself appear: travel out becomes travel back, inside becomes outside, top becomes bottom.

The externalizing locations that an Elmdoner might imagine as giving different perspectives on persons are here seen as attached to persons themselves. People appear to have different locations or positions on their own bodies, and thus different identities according to what they hold in their hands or where the food they eat came form. Things travel to and from them.

Elsewhere, I have described the Melanesian idea of the gift as though it were the anticipated outcome of the transactions which produce it. It at once evokes past transactions and enables those of the future to happen. Gifts themselves take concrete, material forms as shell valuables or pigs, carrying the persons that carry them. The analogy could be extended to other productive activities, to the flutes that both are children and produce children, or spirits that are both within and beyond the body-form of persons. Melanesians have a cultural facility for presenting their extensions of themselves to themselves, a facility for, we could put it, moving without travelling.

The valuable with movement inscribed within (bearing the identities of donor and recipient) or the spirit face that moves up and down a pole are Melanesian cyborgs: a circuit of different figures or components. The components are never equal to what makes them work, which is their centering in the person. This centering might be imagined as a metaphor for perception. It is people's perceptual faculty that grounds 'meaning' and thus forms the circuit of communication between the disparate components. Figures grow and diminish irrespective of their background. They are not equal to that, but they are, one might say, equal to themselves.

The distinction between the Melanesian cyborg and Haraway's half human, half mechanical contraption is that the components of the Melanesian cyborg are conceptually 'cut' from the same material. There is no difference between shell strands and a matrilineage, between a man and a bamboo pole, between a yam and spirit. The one 'is' the other, insofar as they equally evoke the perception of relations. The different components or figures are thus all parts of persons or relationships fixed on to one another. One person or relationship exists cut out of or as an extension of another. Conversely, these extensions — relationships and connections — are integrally part of the person. They are the person's circuit. The effect of the 'same material' produces a perception of the common background to all movement and activity. Hence the further importance of the creative act of severance, the burst of information that makes one person visible as an extended part of another; that makes mother's brothers feel they are only partially connected to their sister's sons, and that differentiates between the locations of the person's identity. The cutting/extension is equally effective, the figures equal to one another in substance, whether the outcome conserves or disregards proportion — whether the result is the dualism of a moiety structure or the enlarged influence of a big man.

Thus it is persons who extend persons. Since they are seemingly made out of the same material, or substance, perhaps such Melanesian figures and their extensions come close to the original idea of mathematical 'remainders' that forever create the possibility of further gaps and thus the further perception of a background to what is present or made known. In terms of the Melanesian cultural imagination, this constant remaindering works to reproduce a grounding sociality of which present relations are only instances, or fractions, and present performances only particulate moments. In Yadran Mimica's (1988) phrasing, the whole is presumed infinite.

The explanation-seeking frames of much Western academic discourse seem at a far remove from this. Yet there **is** a parallel, in one area at least, out of which anthropologists produce the same material each time. The result is palpable, in the solid knowledge that present formulations are only fleeting concepts and present exercises but partial studies. I refer to the writing of anthropology, to the necessary and vitalizing manner in which we produce infinite complexity out of complexity. We become aware of creating more and more gaps. Hence our activities forever magnify a background of potential significance against which — whatever the scale — we try to actualize subtle re-imaginings, and build models that will take everything important into account.

FOOTNOTES

1. A bothersome term, but one necessary to draw attention to the cultural particularity of the ideas here; they form a general background for 'us' social scientists. Haraway (1989:427) offers a nice apology on my behalf. (The apparent solecism of comparing 'Western' and 'Melanesian' discourse is no greater a solecism than, say, differentiating centralized from uncentralized political systems where the very perception of system is intrinsic to the first, extrinsic to the second.) The 'we' in my account is a cultural inclusive; my address is to a Western anthropology, irrespective of whether its particular practitioners are 'Western' or not.

2. I use the term 'perspective' to draw attention to the cultural practice of position-taking, not to endorse a referential or representational interpretation of the 'observer's' relation to 'the world'.

3. Eptiomized as a conjoint problem for the life sciences and social science:

    > the more discretely and specifically we define and bound the units of our study, the more provocative, necessary, and difficult it becomes to account for the relationships among those units; conversely, the more effectively we are able to analyze and sum up the relationships among a set of units, the more provocative, necessary, and difficult it becomes to define the units . . .[A] programme of classification invariably leads into problems involving relationships among the 'types' being identified . . .The alternative . . . has been to capitalize on relationships . . . and speak of continua of species, intermediate types, and emergent phenomena . . . It answers the questions and uncertainties posed by a previous stance of the discipline, but it achieves relational precision at the expense of taxonomic precision (Wagner 1977:385-86).

4. I have in mind the charge of 'navel gazing' so frequently levelled at the introspective. (In Hagen, the cord is cut in such a way as to leave a fleshy globe at the navel's center.)

5. I subsume 'explanation' here. Cf. Peel (1987:89) "Comparison is implicit in any method of deriving understanding through explanation, i.e. by determining the sufficient and necessary conditions for the existence or occurrence of any phenomenon or action" (emphasis

removed). Sufficiency, and thus explanation, is constantly challenge-able by fresh perspectives, as his own argument shows. Peel makes a most convincing case for not being satisfied with anthropological explanations for variations in religious practice in West Africa ("we must recognize the historicity of our ethnographic data").

6. A long and expert literature in philosophy concerns the constancy of material at different scales. I merely gesture towards the discussion in Simons (1987:240f). Whereas something can be in flux — change its parts — by virtue of a change in the proximate matter of which it is made, 'ultimate matter' is defined by its mereological constancy. For if it were to exist, it would always have the same parts. In this view, the "identity of a mass of matter is parasitic upon that of the particles of which it is composed; it is some kind of sum of them" (1987:242). — I am grateful to Gillian Beer for drawing my attention to this work.

7. Barth's analysis is particularly acute on this score. Whether one looks at conception beliefs, cult practices or images of the life-course, one simply replicates innumerable configurations, none of which provides any center, or any overarching set of principles, for the entire 'field'; in this sense there is no field. Disparateness is compounded, he argues, by the incommensurability of the details ethnographers provide.

8. For a quite different set of challenges raised by the concept of scale, see Thornton (1988b).

9. In laying out the development of chaos theory, Gleick observes that as human vision was extended by telescopes and microscopes, the "first discoveries were realizations that each change of scale brought new phenomena and new kinds of behavior" (1988:115). This was to become the natural world of the modernist epoch, of the culture of pluralism where dimensions are like fresh perspectives on phenomena and alter the apprehension of phenomena themselves. As he says, "every extension seems to bring new information" (1988:115). [And, thereby, loss of information too.] But an intriguing problem is set when, as he shows, similar information is reproduced in different scales — as in the famous example of the corrugations of the coast-line, which present the same involute appearance from near or far. That fractal dimensionality should hold an interest in the late twentieth century is a subtext to my text. I find its imagery culturally resonant with the constant reproduction of commercially differentiated goods that are thereby perceived to present all 'the same' choices to the consumer. [A postpluralist loss of perspective.]

10. The 'gap' or image of intervening material 'lost' may or may not be perceptible as a space between. One may equally think of it as ground to figure ('background' to the bursts).

11. The words are borrowed from Ulmer (1985:95), professor of English, citing Owens, the art critic, on the philosopher Derrida. Ulmer speaks of the endeavor not to "abandon or deny reference" but "re-think" reference in another way (1985:87).

12. The elision between ethnographer and anthropologist mirrors that between fieldworker and writer or author. The one person is imagined as moving between these positions. I do not rehearse the arguments that have led to the critique of the fieldworker's authority, though note that Clifford's writings have been particularly influential. The best reference is his recent collection (Clifford 1988).

13. The words are Josephides'. I am grateful to Lisette Josephides for her permission to cite this paper, which includes an extended scrutiny of the initial version of the present exercise.

14. As an art critic, Foster comes from a position where modernism is characterized by a non-representational stance; and postmodernism lies in the denial of a pure aesthetic form with its own internal canons. However, the anthropologist's modernist analog of the pure aesthetic form we call society or culture, objects that required representation, and the contradictions in this exercise have fuelled much of anthropology's energy over the last fifty years. For the ethnographer managed two things simultaneously: describing or representing an object (a society/culture) that was also to be presented in self-sufficient, pure terms. From the outside, such an object was made to appear as internally consistent, holistic, self-referential. Hence it has been a source of some confusion that the resultant 'realism' of this phase of anthropological writing thus appeared out of synchronization with the anti-realism of other forms of modernism. I am grateful to Michael Taussig for pointing this out. I would add that the apparent realism of modernist anthropological reporting depended on making the bizarre appear normal, the fantastic routine (cf. M. Strathern 1987). Insofar as the reader had to break with his own quotidian reality, which had no place in the account, the account was surrealist (cf. Clifford 1988). Reading ethnography in a postmodern way *per contra* allegedly restores the reality of the fantastic.

15. Webster (1987:50-51) calls this presentation cultural aestheticism.

16. Juxtaposition operates like a single scale, where all otherness is understood as of the same order (Rabinow 1983).

17. Parkin (1987:53) provides an arresting example of serial contexts, each the 're-working' of its predecessor, which each time puts us into a fresh world. The positions are related to one another, and it is, he argues, epistemologically wasteful to jettison insights gained from previous positions.

18. "And the point, we believe, of these provocations for anthropologists is not so much to change writing practices radically . . . as to change the conditions of reception of anthropological work" (Tyler and Marcus 1987:277).

19. Clifford writes *apropos* the essays: "If they are postanthropological, they are also post-literary" (1986:5).

20. Roth's (1989) critique, that refuses the gesture towards political sensitivity on the grounds that writing privileges writing, is an example of one such counter-criticism. Like Moeran (1988), Roth also comments that Clifford and Marcus overlook their own strategies.

21. The questions here were posed by Jukka Siikala, Nigel Rapport and Richard Fardon respectively. James Weiner points out that the distinction between representation and evocation is in any case tendentious and rhetorical itself.

22. The question is posed by Gillian Beer (1989), in a provocative lecture that draws among other things on the semi-tragic return of Jemmy Button to his native Tierra del Fuego whence he was taken in 1830 by Captain Fitzroy, later captain of **The Beagle**. Fitzroy and Darwin witnessed his return in 1833, and he was sighted again some fifteen years later. As it was relayed, she remarks, the tale of Jemmy Button is also a tale of Victorian interpretation and counter-interpretation.

23. Beer is at this point citing Said's **Orientalism**. She immediately follows the comment with the observation that "the assumptions of the home culture and language imbue what can be seen, and pre-conditions what can be valued [by the traveller]. But **these assumptions are also always contested** . . . within the current language of the [home] tribe" (1989:8, my emphasis). This position leads into my next section.

24. Hannerz's (1988) terminology for a new perception of the kinds of hybrid cultures produced by modern communications and charac-

terized by an intercontinental traffic in meaning:

> we need words which do not carry the negative load of
> a term like 'hybrid', and points of view which help us
> conceptualize the interconnections and the emergence
> of new forms and units within world culture instead of
> leading our thoughts astray.

There is a rapidly growing literature on cosmopolitanism, transnational networks and tourism (e.g. Crick 1988).

25. After Beer's (1989) disquisition on Thomas Hardy's **The Return of the Native**. The returning native is received as an outcast.

26. The references to Durham and Hulme were inspired by brief conversations with Huw Beynon and Peter Marcus. Bouquet (1985; 1986; n.d.) has explored the differences which Essex Elmdoners make so salient within their village alongside the Devon family farm with its internal division between the farmer and the farmer's wife who takes in guests. As is also true among the 'real' Elmdoners, she comments that the presence of strangers is an accommodation of other divisions, not the cause of them. The interest of her material is the replication of these 'similar ideas' on such a minute scale — the single farm, at once a natural entity and an outwardly oriented business organization prepared to have strangers live there.

27. In Haraway's words (1988:581):

> The visualizing technologies are without apparent limit.
> The eye of any ordinary primate like us can be endlessly
> enhanced by sonography systems, magnetic resonance
> imaging, artificial intelligence-linked graphic manipula-
> tion systems, scanning electron microscopes, computed
> tomography scanners, color enhancement techniques,
> satellite surveillance systems, home and office video display
> terminals, cameras for every purpose from filming the
> mucous membrane lining the gut cavity of a marine worm
> living in the vent gases on a fault between continental
> plates to mapping a planetary hemisphere elsewhere in
> the solar system.

28. Compare, for example, Nye (1987) on Kristeva's critique of Derrida, and Flax's (1987) claim for a substantive relation between deconstruction and feminist theories of gender relations. One comes from

a Department of Philosophy, the other a Department of Political Science. There is also an established counter position which regards postmodernism as the 'death throes' of the male aesthetic and which challenges women to produce cultural forms without recourse to the strategies of deconstruction (e.g. Lee 1987).

29. Cf. DuBois *et al.* (1985:2) on the "essential duality of feminist scholarship — that it is rooted simultaneously in the disciplinary structures of contemporary intellectual inquiry and in a social movement."

30. A cyborg, we may note, does not recognize coherence or opposition or hierarchy (Crick 1985:72-73, the three manifestations of sign systems).

31. I use the 'tool' here as a trope for 'culture' in Ingold's sense, that is, a vehicle for social life translating "social purpose into practical effectiveness" (1986:262). In reference to the discussion that follows, I note that a tool is neither body nor machine.

32. Haraway (1986:89) connects in this way two areas of contemporary primatologial discourse — science and myth:

> Like the boundaries between nature and culture, sex and gender, animal and human, the scientific and mythic characters of primate discourses are not quite in phase. They evoke each other, echo each other, annoy each other, but are not identical to each other. Science and myth neither exclude nor replace each other.

33. The comment is from Susan Fleming, and I am grateful for her critique.

34. I run their account of 'tourists' and 'travellers' together. The travellers travel light and adventurously distinguish themselves from tourists by criteria very similar to those an anthropologist might use to distinguish him or herself from both. Tourists, Errington and Gewertz (1989) observe, have little impetus or competence to go beyond self-reference.

35. Thanks to Nigel Rapport for showing me this paper. Biersack (1989) makes the point that there is nothing uniquely anthropological about 'cultural analysis.'

36. They add that in stratified societies it may be necessary to have

different codes for "each stratum." They hint at future possibilities of producing cross-cultural data sets that even incorporate "individual-level data" (Burton and White 1987:145).

37. As for instance articulated in the interpretist realization that ethnography "does not produce data, bits of information that are then fed into, and used up by, analytical machinery; what we take away from the field are texts, documents of communicative events, of performances and conversations" (Fabian 1985:19).

38. Because it appears to offer the conditions for 'controlled comparison,' an assumption common in discursive practice. In statistical practice, probability sampling procedures deliberately attempt to overcome the effects of temporal or spatial propinquity.

> [T]he alternative to sampling is the continuous-area approach where data are coded for all of the societies in a region . . In the past this was seen as antithetical to the goals of causal analysis, because of Galton's problem. The recent solutions to Galton's problem obviate this objection to continous-area samples by making the study of intersocietal connections a part of the research program (Burton and White 1987:146).

Continuous-area analysis has a long history of its own (the difference between probability sampling and continuous-area sampling can be traced back to the divergent interests of Tylor and Boas). See the discussion in J. Jorgensen (1970:320-329), and of his own work in culture area taxonomy (where he derived a taxonomy for 172 western North American Indian societies on the basis of 292 variables, making a total of 1,577 attributes; eight major topics of culture were covered, ranging from 30-45 variables per topic).

39. I exaggerate, but not entirely, having offered a contrast between initiation practices in two Highlands societies in terms of an internal correlation with the requirements of the political systems in each (M. Strathern 1985). What hangs 'between' in this case is the unspoken analog: that initiation practice and political form **will** co-vary — that I can use an internal relationship in one society as a cross-cultural device — that is , assume that the same internal relationship will hold elsewhere.

40. However, Robert Thornton (in a draft version of Thornton 1988a) points out that the contrast between 'finding' connections and 'making'

them is an old-established one in philosophy, after the respective classificatory projects of Aristotle and Kant.

41.   He freely draws other parallels between episodes in the performances and incidents in the story. For example, take the images of the dancers under their swaying bamboo poles.

> One cannot help thinking of that image of creation of the old mountain Papuan culture in which men had been formed from the blood of the *Nsit*-bird [here as a variant on the pigeon?], and at the end of the creative process stood wet and red with blood at the foot of the tall bamboo poles which had burst in the heat (1963:93).

On other occasions, the people he was with made connections (1963:110).

> A multitude of spectators, laughing and chatting, are crowded round the open space. Suddenly the women of the lineages taking part appear on the dancing-place. They have hung string bags on their backs, with the handles knotted together on the head . . . In their hands they carry small canes of bamboo . . . It was explained that [the] sound [they make] imitated the call of that primordial pigeon, to which the Old Man had changed himself, and from whose blood mankind was finally formed. It was also added that hunters, too, make use of such an instrument, to allure a kind of pigeon which responds to the call.

42.   The inappropriate excision echoes Young's (1987) tragic story of the man who tried to cut a boar's tusk pendant from a woman's living breast.

43.   The necklace is not just an icon of a journey, but of the matrilineage, the relation between them, and the procreative potency of interaction. For instance:

> the necklace [can be] viewed as a circular path, broken in the centre by a clasp which is sometimes a buzzard's beak (symbolic of death), sometimes a 'canoe-shaped' gold-lip shell, but either way a symbol of bridging. Indeed, if each 'line' or side is viewed as the 'line' of matrilineage, it is a short leap to suggest that each red disc is a woman

at different points along a life-path spanning marriage
and death.

[Moreover]
the red shell discs that [combine] with the white shell
head display the colours of procreation. Thus it is not
at all unlikely that the head . . . represents a new ancestral
individual, with a 'voice' of chiming shells to announce
that the [necklace] is ritually alive, and to render visually
the emanating sound of the newborn. We could even
speculate that the head is emerging from between the
legs of the matrilineage (Battaglia 1983:300-301, Sabarl
terms omitted).

44. Gourley himself (e.g. 1975:38) offers a most sophisticated critique
of conventional typologies of these instruments.

45. For one design, he comments (1963:94):

[a]t first glance the upper band appears as a strip of
black in which white rhomboids have been left standing.
Yet if one looks more closely at the black parts remaining,
one sees that they are shaped like an hour-glass. They
are indeed stated to represent drums. We must understand them as the simplified outline of the constricted
drums all men of the Wantoat valley play in the cult and
for dancing. The white rhomboids are called *banip*. This
word is really a general term for the inside of a body.
In this indefinite sense it is also used for belly.

46. Bamboo wind instruments play a negligible role in cult life. Although
flutes are sounded in some ritual contexts, one could not talk of
a sacred flute complex of the kind Hays has identified for other parts
of the Highlands.

47. Prompted by Anthony Cohen's observations after hearing Howard
Morphy read a paper on Arnhem Land bark paintings with their
equivocal positioning of spears and digging sticks.

48. A suggestion from Robert Foster (pers. comm.), and see Foster (1985).

49. I use 'image' to refer both to the sense impression of perception
and to the conceived, elicited forms of sense impressions such as
'a figure' or 'pattern'.

50. Gell's discussion at this point is on the cassowary mask with which the festival sequence opens, also the point of departure for much of his analysis.

51. The unit involved is a clan segment, but Gell follows Umeda shorthand here (1975:49 etc.).

52. On the surface, there appears no reciprocity, for women make the principal bags which men elaborate, and make them unaided. However, the food women grow and are grown by comes from land prepared by and identified with men, and it is from this male 'support' that they do their female tasks. Specifically: "The male recipient must make continuous returns to compensate the work of his sister's/mother's/wife's hands. Thus, when a man uses his feather elaborated string bag to return hunted food to the donor of the principal form he nourishes both the woman and their relationship" (Mackenzie 1986:22).

53. I am grateful for permission to draw so extensively from her work before it is published.

54. However, the provenance of the feathers also 'encloses' the boys within the maternal care of their initiators:

> the boy's [initiation bag] was traditionally elaborated with wild fowl feathers. During the first initiation ceremony initiates were traditionally enclosed within small huts and subjected to fierce heat treatments whilst attached to the roof with long vines. The symbolism of this scene is linked with the nesting habits of the wild fowl, for the male of *Megapodius sp.* incubates the eggs utilizing heat from mounds of rotting vegetation . . .The vines could be interpreted as umbilical cords within a surrogate communal womb, the initiation hut, which by analogy functions like a woman's string bag as a protective container for collective rather than individual reproduction. The link between initiation house, surrogate womb and the string bag is made quite explicit by the fact that the small round doorway to the men's house is said to be 'like the mouth of a string bag' (B. Craig, pers. comm.) (Mackenzie in press).

55. While they do not produce for an external market, Telefol women 'import' certain **additional** features from elsewhere in Papua New

Guinea (and from beyond the Ok area). Conversely, they adhere to their traditional features in the **basic** working of the bag, which are the very features they have 'exported' to other Mountain Ok women. (For a detailed study of the relationship between changing trading practice and enmity/amity in other relations elsewhere, see Gewertz 1983.)

56. Mackenzie here acknowledges Dan Jorgensen's work in Telefolmin.

57. Gardner makes an analytical point about the significance Mianmin place on the effectiveness of action. Particular forms of rites are the means to an end, and different peoples have different means, as Mianmin themselves compare them. I quote (1983:354-5):

> [a Mianmin] highlander had been acting as my translator during an interview with a lowlands big-man about initiation rituals among his group. The lowlander had given me an account of a very short, small-scale rite which bore the same name as one of the major ceremonies performed by the highlanders. Later I asked my translator what he thought of the account. . . He replied . . .'But look at this man. His taro grows well, he kills wild pigs and cassowaries and his skin is strong. His ancestors look after him just as our ancestors look after us.'

Errington and Gewertz (1986:107) comment that Chambri believe they are following similar ritual procedures in effecting contact with the ancestors whether the ancestral point of origin is Chambri or (through import) a neighboring population.

58. The management and creation of 'loss' is treated explicitly in Battaglia (1990). Deborah Gewertz draws my attention to the parallel in Chambri, where the availability of power is seen to diminish with each generation, spurring men to compete among themselves in an escalating demand for it (Errington and Gewertz 1986).

59. From the Bolovip point of view, Baktaman initiation rites are regarded as similar but not identical (1987:24). Barth cites D. Jorgensen's account of Telefolmin practice at a later point (1987:51) to show [but not in these words] that 'red' is for the Telefol a version of 'white' (menstrual blood is revealed as the source of white bone, and what is separated at one moment is brought together at another). On the further relativity of men's and women's perspectives, see Annette Weiner's (1982) discussion of Bimin-Kuskusmin.

60. I do not mean to evoke information theory; for the analog computer there are no 'gaps' in the system, and for the digital, 'absence' is information. My language does not observe these differences.

61. Mackenzie amplifies the story (see Gardner 1983:358) about Telefol having dropped an initial initiation stage after a tragedy in which initiates were killed and their female relatives committed suicide. The term for the string bag boys wore in that initial stage is used for what has now become the 'first stage', and gives, we might surmise, the former 'second stage' bag a double meaning as indicating both former and present first stage initiation.

62. After Harrison 1984. (Feil himself notes a similar oscillation for Maring (1987:50) and makes an interesting contrast between continuous and discontinuous production over the horticultural year.)

63. This is not the place to quarrel with his judgements. On the first point, obvious counter-arguments lie in Joesphides' (1985) thesis; on the second, in several publications by Andrew Strathern (e.g. 1982 ed.).

64. See Schwimmer (n.d.) on a similar point in relation to Goffman's work. Howe (1987:150) notes that we do not really compare 'societies' or 'data', but compare interpretations of data, so the relations between data are always the 'joint constructions' of many anthropologists.

65. His problem is that

> there is no compelling technological (material) link . . . between the shape of an Anga arrow, the transverse section of the bow which shoots it, the ground-plan of the house where the hunter lives, the use or non-use of bark-capes or the order of the operations for opening a new garden. Nevertheless, among the Anga these various technological traits share approximately the same non-random distributions. In other words, everything happens **as if** the local forms of these physically independent technological traits were systematically associated with one another (1989:159, original emphasis).

The various explanations that come to mind — that these differences serve as ethnic markers, are the outcome of specializations in production in the context of inter-group trade, or are related to sustaining the opposition of male and female worlds — do not themselves comprise a single logical order.

66. And thus replicates individual units. Ingold's critique of Lévi-Strauss's *bricoleur* is along these lines, "an animated assemblage of cultural elements" (1986:200). In its place, Ingold (1986:293) argues that we need some concept of a 'person' whose conscious life is a movement that adopts culture as a vehicle.

67. Clifford invokes Aimé Césaire, who invents a neologistic cultural politics from the inventiveness of a hybrid and heteroglot Caribbean world. The poet forces his readers, Clifford observes (1988:175), to construct meanings from the debris of historical and future possibilities. Clifford intends us to see a hopeful inventory, by contrast with Lévi-Strauss' global vision. The latter's narrative of entropy turns on the questionable Eurocentrism of scholarship gathering up a unified human history, "memorializing the world's local historicities" (1988:14-15).

68. In the composition of the present ornamental strip this so-called *banip* [belly] design only appeared in the second place, for obviously the first idea was to set up a horizontal row of drums. But once the *banip* form had thus been incidentally shaped, a . . . name was also given to the unintended design, opening the possibility of reading any kind of meaning into this more or less secondary design.
From the beginning, [the native] only sees the outlines of the drums, and is well aware that the white parts have simply remained open . . . The upper row of ornamentation is not a black band in which white rhomboids have been left open, but a white band which has been filled with drum-designs. The thin lines within the white rhomboids do not trace the outline of the rhomboid but that of the drums. Now if the native, questioned, has to decide whether the white patches have any meaning, he remembers similar designs and very logically comes to the neutral term of *banip*, inside of a body. (Schmitz 1963:94).

69. Each place where initiation is held comprises a ritual center. So in a sense, the management of each initiation stage comprises a 'ritual center' and, indeed, so does each secret bundle. Barth describes how experts in Bolovip discussed the Mafom initiation stage. The acknowledged leader (reluctantly) brought out his secret bundle, and

proceeded with his detailed account of the ten-day main

ritual, showing occasional (correct) comparative knowledge of the corresponding Baktaman rite and also of
some other local variants . . .The full contents of his
Mafom bundle was, however, never exposed; and some
parts of the ritual were also kept secret. [Another leader
present] confirmed that parts were also unknown to him;
he would be able to produce a Mafom initiation but only
in its major outline and therefore with reduced or
questionable efficacy. At no point did the description
or ensuing conversation turn into an explanation or
exegesis of the rite; it remained throughout a rendering
of the initiation itself: its events, acts, and equipment
(1987:25).

REFERENCES

Appadurai, Arjun
  1986 Theory in Anthropology: Center and Periphery. **Comp. Studies in Society & History** 28:356-61.

Barth, Fredrik
  1987 **Cosmologies in the Making. A Generative Approach to Cultural Variation in New Guinea**. Cambridge: Cambridge University Press.

Battaglia, Debbora
  1983 Projecting Personhood in Melanesia: The Dialectics of Artefact Symbolism on Sabarl Island. **Man** (n.s.) 18:289-304.

Battaglia, Debbora
  1990 **On the Bones of the Serpent: Person, Memory and Mortality in Sabarl Island Society**. Chicago: University of Chicago Press.

Beer, Gillian
  1989 **Can the Native Return?** The Hilda Hume Lecture for 1988. London: University of London.

Biersack, Aletta
  1982 Ginger Gardens for the Ginger Woman: Rites and Passages in a Melanesian Society. **Man** (n.s.) 17:239-258.

Biersack, Aletta
  1989 Local Knowledge, Local History: Geertz and Beyond. In **The New Cultural History**, L. Hunt (ed.). Berkeley and Los Angeles: California University Press.

Boon, James A.
  1982 **Other Tribes, Other Scribes. Symbolic Anthropology in the Comparative Study of Cultures, Histories, Religions, and Texts**. Cambridge: Cambridge University Press.

Boon, James A.
  1986 Between-the-Wars Bali: Rereading the Relics. In **Malinowski, Rivers, Benedict and Others, History of Anthropology** IV, G. Stocking (ed.). University of Wisconsin Press.

Bouquet, Mary
  1985 **Family, Servants and Visitors. The Farm Household in Nineteenth and Twentieth Century Devon**. Norwich: Geo Books.

Bouquet, Mary
  1986 'You Cannot be a Brahmin in the English Countryside.' The Partition
  ing of Status, and its Representation within the Family Farm in Devon. In
  Symbolising Boundaries, A. P. Cohen (ed.). Manchester: Manchester
  University Press.

Bouquet, Mary
  n.d. Two Tribes on the Family Farm: A Nineteen Eighties' Encounter
  Between Sociology and Anthropology [manuscript, 1985].

Burridge, Kenelm
  1979 **Somone, No One. An Essay on Individuality**. Princeton: Princton
  University Press.

Burton, Michael L. and Douglas R. White
  1987 Cross-Cultural Surveys Today. **Annual Review of Anthropology**
  16:143-60.

Christiansen, Palle Ove
  1988 Construction and Consumption of the Past: From 'Montaillou' to
  'The Name of the Rose. **Ethnologia Europaea** 18:2-24.

Clifford, James
  1986 Partial Truths. Introduction to **Writing Culture**, J. Clifford and G.E.
  Marcus (eds.). Berkeley and Los Angeles: California University Press.

Clifford, James
  1988 **The Predicament of Culture: Twentieth Century Ethnography,
  Literature, and Art**. Cambridge, Mass.: Harvard University Press.

Clifford, James and Marcus, George (eds.)
  1986 **Writing Culture: The Poetics and Politics of Ethnography**. Berkeley
  and Los Angeles: University of California Press.

Cohen, Anthony P.
  1985 **The Symbolic Construction of Community**. London: Tavistock
  Publications.

Cohen, Anthony P.
  1986 Of Symbols and Boundaries, or, Does Ertie's Greatcoat Hold the Key?
  In **Symbolising Boundaries**, A.P. Cohen (ed.). Manchester: Manchester
  University Press.

Cohen, Anthony P.
  1987 **Whalsay. Symbol, Segment and Boundary in a Shetland Island Com**
  munity. Manchester: Manchester University Press.

Crapanzano, Vincent
  1985 **Waiting: The Whites of South Africa.** New York: Random House.

Crick, Malcolm
  1985 'Tracing' the Anthropological Self: Quizzical Reflections on
  Fieldwork, Tourism and the Ludic. **Social Analysis** 17:71-92.

Crick, Malcolm
  1988 Sun, Sex, Sights, and Servility: Representations of International
  Tourism in the Social Sciences. CHAI (**Criticism, Heresy and Interpreta**
  tion) 1:37-76.

Currie, Dawn and Hamida Kazi
  1987 Academic Feminism and the Process of De-Radicalization: Re-examin-
  ing the Issues. **Feminist Review** 25:77-98.

DuBois, Ellen Carol **et al.**
  1985 **Feminist Scholarship: Kindling in the Groves of Academe.** Urbana:
  University of Illinois Press.

Eistenstein, Hester
  1984 **Contemporary Feminst Thought.** Sydney: Unwin Paperbacks.

Errington, Frederick and Deborah Gewertz
  1986 The Confluence of Powers: Entropy and Importation among the
  Chambri. **Oceania** 57:99-113.

Errington, Frederick and Deborah Gewertz
  1987 On Unfinished Dialogues and Paper Pigs. **American Ethnologist**
  14:367-376.

Errington, Frederick and Deborah Gewertz
  1989 Tourism and Anthropology in a Post-Modern World. **Oceania**
  60:37-54.

Fabian, Johannes
  1983 **Time and the Other. How Anthropology Makes its Object.** New York:
  Columbia University Press.

Fabian, Johannes
1985 Culture, Time, and the Object of Anthropology. **Berkshire Review**
20:7-23.

Fabian, Johannes
n.d. Presence and Representation: The Other and Anthropological Writing.
[Paper presented to American Anthropological Association Meeting,
Philadelphia, 1986.]

Fardon, Richard
1987 'African Ethnogenesis' , Limits to the Comparability of Ethnic
Phenomena. In **Comparative Ethnology,** L. Holy (ed.). Oxford: Basil
Blackwell.

Fardon, Richard (ed.)
1990 **Regional Traditions in Ethnographic Writing. Localizing Strategies.**
Washington: Smithsonian Institution Press.

Feil, Daryl K.
1987 **The Evolution of Highland Papua New Guinea Societies.** Cambridge :
Cambridge University Press.

Feld, Steven
1982 **Sound and Sentiment. Birds, Weeping, Poetics, and Song in Kaluli
Expression.** Philadelphia: University of Pennsylvania Press.

Flax, Jane
1987 Postmodernism and Gender Relations in Feminist Theory. **Signs:
Journal of Women in Culture and Society** 12:621-643.

Foster, Hal
1985 Postmodernism. A Preface to **Postmodern Culture,** H. Foster (ed.).
London: Pluto Press.

Foster, Robert J.
1985 Producion and Value in the Enga Tee. **Oceania** 55:182-96.

Friedman, Jonathan
1987 Beyond Otherness or: The Spectacularization of Anthropology. **Telos**
71:161-70.

Friedman, Jonathan
1988 Commentary on Sangren, 'Rhetoric and the Authority of
Anthropology.' **Current Anthropology** 29:426-7.

Game, Ann
   1985 Review Essay (on Hester Eisenstein's 'Contemporary Feminist
      Thought' and Clare Burton's 'Subordination: Feminism and Socal
      Theory). **Australian Feminist Studies** 1:129-139.

Gardner, Don S.
   1983 Performativity in Ritual: The Mianmin Case. **Man** (n.s.) 18:346-360.

Gell, Alfred
   1975 **Metamorphosis of the Cassowaries: Umeda Society, Language and
      Ritual**. London: The Athlone Press.

Gewertz, Deborah B.
   1983 **Sepik River Societies. A Historical Ethnography of the Chambri and
      their Neighbors.** New Haven: Yale University Press.

Gewertz, Deborah B. (ed.)
   1988 **Myths of Matriarchy Reconsidered**. Sydney: Oceania Monograph 33.

Gewertz, Deborah and Edward Schieffelin (eds.)
   1985 **History and Ethnohistory in Papua New Guinea**. Sydney: Oceania
      Monograph 28.

Gillison, Gillian
   1980 Images of Nature in Gimi Thought. In **Nature, Culture and Gender,**
      C. MacCormack and M. Strathern (eds.). Cambridge: Cambridge
      University Press.

Gillison, Gillian
   1987 Incest and the Atom of Kinship: The Role of the Mother's Brother in
      a New Guinea Highlands Society. **Ethos** 15:166-202.

Gillison, Gillian
   In press The Flute Myth and the Law of Equivalence: Origins of a Principle
      of Exchange. In **Big Men and Great Men. The Development of a Compari-
      son in Melanesia**, M. Godelier and M. Strathern (eds.) Cambridge:
      Cambridge University Press.

Gleick, James
   1988 [1987] **Chaos: Making a New Science**. London: Heinemann.

Godelier, Maurice
   1986 (Trans. R. Swyer [1982]) **The Making of Great Men. Male Domination and Power among the New Guinea Baruya**. Cambridge: Cambridge University Press.

Godelier, Maurice and Marilyn Strathern (eds.)
   In press **Big Men and Great Men: Personificatons of Power in Melanesia**. Cambridge: Cambridge University Press.

Gourlay, K.A.
   1975 Sound-producing Instruments in Traditional Society: A Study of Esoteric Instruments and Their role in Male-Female Relations. **New Guinea Research Bulletin** 60. Canberra and Port Moresby: Australian National University.

Hannerz, Ulf
   1986 Theory in Anthropology: Small is Beautiful? The Problem of Complex Cultures. **Compar. Stud. Soc. and History** 28:362-67.

Hannerz, Ulf
   1988 American Culture: Creolized, Creolizing. In **American Culture: Creolized. Creolizing,** E. Asard (ed.). Uppsala: Swedish Inst. North American Studies.

Hannerz, Ulf
   1990 Cosmopolitans and Locals in World Culture. **Theory, Culture and Society** 7:211-225.

Haraway, Donna
   1985 A Manifesto for Cyborgs: Science, Technology, and Socialist Feminism in the 1980s. **Socialist Review** 80:65-107.

Haraway, Donna
   1986 Primatology is Politics by Other Means. In **Feminist Approaches to Science,** Ruth Bleier (ed.). New York: Pergamon Press.

Haraway, Donna
   1988 Situated Knowledges: The Science Question in Feminism and the Privilege of Partial Perspective. **Feminist Studies** 14:575-99.

Haraway, Donna
   1989 **Primate Visions: Gender, Race, and Nature in the World of Modern Science**. New York: Routledge.

Harding, Sandra
  1986 The Instability of the Analytical Categories of Feminist Theory. **Signs: Journal of Women in Culture and Science** 11:645-664.

Harrison, Simon
  1984 New Guinea Highland Social Structure in a Lowland Totemic Mythology. **Man** (n.s.) 19:389-403.

Hastrup, Kirsten
  n.d. Writing Ethnography: State of the Art. [Paper presented to ASA Annual Conference, Anthropology and Autobiography. York, 1989.]

Hawkesworth, Mary E.
  1989 Knowers, Knowing, Known: Feminist Theory and Claims of Truth. **Signs: Journal of Women in Culture and Science** 14:533-557.

Hays, Terence E.
  1986 Sacred Flutes, Fertility, and Growth in the Papua New Guinea Highlands. **Anthropos** 81:435-53.

Hays, Terence E.
  1988 'Myths of Matriarchy' and the Sacred Flute Complex of the Papua New Guinea Highlands. In **Myths of Matriarchy Reconsidered**, D. Gewertz (ed.). Sydney: Oceania Monograph 33.

Herdt, Gilbert H. (ed.)
  1984 **Ritualized Homosexuality in Melanesia**. Berkeley and Los Angeles: University of California Press.

Holy, Ladislav (ed.)
  1987 **Comparative Anthropology**. Oxford: Basil Blackwell.

Howe, Leo
  1987 Caste in Bali and India: Levels of Comparison. In **Comparative Anthropology**, L. Holy (ed.). Oxford: Basil Blackwell.

Ingold, Tim
  1986 **Evolution and Social Life**. Cambridge: Cambridge University Press.

Ingold, Tim
  1988 Tools, Minds and Machines: An Excursion in the Philosophy of Technology. **Techniques et culture** 12:151-176.

Jackson, Michael
1987 On Ethnographic Truth. **Canberra Anthropology** 10:1-31.

Jameson, Fredric
1985 Postmodernism and Consumer Society. In **Postmodern Culture,**
H. Foster (ed.). London and Sydney: Pluto Press.

Jorgensen, Dan
1985 Femsep's Last Garden: A Telefol Response to Mortality. In **Aging and
its Transformations: Moving Towards Death in Pacific Societies,** D.A. and
D.R. Counts (eds.). ASAO Monograph 10. Lanham: University Press of
America.

Jorgensen, Joseph G.
1979 Cross-cultural Comparisons. **Annual Review of Anthropology** 8:309-31.

Josephides, Lisette
1985 **The Production of Inequality. Gender and Exchange among the Kewa.**
London: Tavistock Publications.

Josephides, Lisette
n.d. Postmodernism in Melanesia. [Paper presented at Melanesian Research
Group Seminar, convenors L. Josephides and E. Hirsch, London School
of Economics, 1988.]

Juillerat, Bernard
1986 **Les enfants du sang. Société, reproduction et imaginaire en Nouvelle-
Guinée.** Paris: Editions de la Maison des Sciences de l'Homme.

Juillerat, Bernard
In press **Shooting the Sun: Ritual and Meaning in the West Sepik: Ida
Revisited.** Washington: Smithsonian Institution Press.

Keesing, Roger M.
1982 Introduction to **Rituals of Manhood, Male Initiation in Papua New
Guinea,** G.H. Herdt (ed.). Berkeley: University of California Press.

Leach, Jerry W. and Edmund R. Leach (eds.)
1983 **The Kula. New Perspectives on Massim Exchange.** Cambridge: Cambridge University Press.

Lederman, Rena
1986a **What Gifts Engender: Social Relations and Politics in Mendi, High
land Papua New Guinea.** Cambridge: Cambridge University Press.

Lederman, Rena
1986b Changing Times in Mendi: Notes Towards Writing Highland and New Guinea History. **Ethnohistory** 33:1-30.

Lee, Rosa
1987 Resisting Amnesia: Feminism, Painting and Postmodernism. **Feminist Review** 26:5-28.

Lemonnier, Pierre
1989 Bark Capes, Arrowheads and Concorde: On Social Representations of Technology. In **The Meaning of Things: Material Culture and Symbolic Expression**, I. Hodder (ed.). London: Unwin Hyman.

Mackenzie, Maureen A.
1986 The Bilum is Mother of Us All. An Interpretative Analysis of the Social Value of the Telefol Looped String Bag. M.A. Thesis. Canberra: The Australian National University [to be published by Harwood Academic].

Mackenzie, Maureen A.
In press The Telefol String Bag: A Cultural Object with Androgynous Forms. In **Children of Afek: Tradition and Change among the Mountain-Ok of Central New Guinea**, B. Craig and D. Hyndman (eds.). Sydney: Oceania Monographs.

Marcus, George E. (ed.) with A. Appadurai
1988 Place and Voice in Anthropological Theory. **Cultural Anthropology** (spec. issue) 3.

Mimica, Jadran
1988 **Intimations of Infinity: The Cultural Meanings of the Iqwaye Counting System and Number**. Oxford: Berg.

Moeran, Brian
1988 Of Chrystanthemums and Swords: Problems in Ethnographic Writing. CHAI **(Criticsm, Heresy and Interpretation)** 1:1-17.

Moi, Toril
1985 **Sexual/Textual Politics: Feminst Literary Theory**. London: Routledge.

Moore, Henrietta
1988 **Feminism and Anthropology**. Cambridge: Polity Press.

Mosko, Mark
  1988 **Quadrpartitie Structure. Categories, Relations and Homologies in Bush Mekeo Culture**. Cambridge: Cambridge University Press.

Munn, Nancy D.
  1983 Gawan Kula: Spatiotemporal Control and the Symbolism of Influence. In **New Perspectives on the Kula**, E. and J. Leach (eds.). Cambridge: Cambridge University Press.

Munn, Nancy D.
  1986 **The Fame of Gawa. A Symbolic Study of Value Transformation in a Massim (Papua New Guinea) Society**. Cambridge: Cambridge University Press.

Nye, Andrew
  1987 Women Clothed with the Sun: Julia Kristeva and the Escape from/to Language. **Signs: Journal of Women in Culture and Society** 12: 664-686.

Ong, Aihwa
  1987a Disassembling Gender in an Electronics Age [Review Essay]. **Feminist Studies** 13:609-626.

Ong, Aihwa
  1987b **Spirits of Resistance and Capitalist Discipline: Factory Women in Malaysia**. Albany: State University of New York Press.

Overing, Joanna
  1987 Translation as a Creative Process: The Power of the Name. In **Comparative Anthropology**, L. Holy (ed.). Oxford: Basil Blackwell.

Owens, Craig
  1985 The Discourse of Others: Feminists and Postmodernism. In **Postmodern Culture**, H. Foster (ed.). London & Sydney: Pluto Press.

Paige, K.E. and J. M. Paige
  1981 **The Politics of Reproductive Ritual**. Berkeley/Los Angeles: University of California Press.

Parkin, David
  1987 Comparison as the Search for Continuity. In **Comparative Anthropology**, L. Holy (ed.). Oxford: Basil Blackwell.

Peel, John D.Y.
1987 History, Culture and the Comparative Method: A West African Puzzle. In **Comparative Anthropology**, L. Holy (ed.). Oxford: Basil Blackwell

Rabinow, Paul
1983 Humanism as Nihilism: The Bracketing of Truth and Seriousness in American Cultural Anthropology. In **Social Behavior and Moral Enquiry**, R. Bellah *et al.* (eds.). New York: Columbia University Press.

Rabinow, Paul
1986 Representations are Social Facts. In **Writing Culture: The Poetics and Politics of Ethnography,** J. Clifford and G. Marcus (eds.). Berkeley and Los Angeles: University of California Press.

Rapport, Nigel
1986 Cedar High Farm: Ambiguous Symbolic Boundary. An Essay in Anthropological Intuition. In **Symbolising Boundaries**, A.P. Cohen (ed.). Manchester: Manchester University Press.

Rapport, Nigel
n.d. Passage to Britain: A Sterotypical View of Coming Home from the Old World to the New. [University of Manchester, manuscript.]

Rosman, Abraham and Rubel, Paula G.
1978 **Your Own Pigs You May Not Eat: A Comparative Study of New Guinea Societies**. Chicago: Chicago University Press.

Roth, Paul A.
1989 Ethnography Without Tears. **Current Anthropology** 30.

Salmond, Anne
1982 Theoretical Landscapes. On a Cross-Cultural Conception of Knowledge. In **Semantic Anthropology**, D. Parkin (ed.). London: Academic Press.

Sangren, Steven P.
1988 Rhetoric and the Authority of Ethnography: 'Post Modernism' and the Social Reproduction of Texts. **Current Anthropology** 29:405-435.

Schmitz, Carl A.
1963 **Wantoat: Art and Religion of the Northeast New Guinea Papuans**. The Hague: Mouton & Co.

Schwimmer, Eric
  n.d. The Anthropology of the Interaction Order. [Université Laval, Quebec,
  manuscript.]

Sillitoe, Paul
  1988 **Made in Niugini: Technology in the Highlands of Papua New Guinea**.
  London: British Museum Publications.

Simons, Peter
  1987 **Parts: A Study in Ontology**. Oxford: Clarendon Press.

Stacey, Judith
  1988 Can There be a Feminist Ethnography? **Women's Studies
  International Forum** 11:21-27.

Stanley, Liz and Sue Wise
  1983 **Breaking Out: Feminist Consciousness and Feminist Research**.
  London: Routledge and Kegan Paul.

Stocking, George W.
  1987 **Victorian Anthropology**. New York: The Free Press.

Strathern, Andrew J. (ed.)
  1982 **Inequality in New Guinea Highlands Societies**. Cambridge:
  Cambridge University Press.

Strathern, Marilyn
  1981 **Kinship at the Core: An Anthropology of Elmdon, a village in
  North-West Sussex, in the 1960s**. Cambridge: Cambridge University Press.

Strathern, Marilyn
  1985 Knowing Power and Being Equivocal: Three Melanesain Contexts. In
  Power and Knowledge: Anthropological and Sociological Perspectives, R.
  Fardon (ed.). Edinburgh; Scottish Academic Press.

Strathern, Marilyn
  1986 An Awkward Relationship: The Case of Feminism and Anthropology.
  Signs: Journal of Women's Culture and Society 12:276-292.

Strathern, Marilyn
  1987 Out of Context: The Persuasive Fictions of Anthropology. **Current
  Anthropology** 28:251:281.

Strathern Marilyn
  1989 Between a Melanesianist and a Deconstructive Feminist. **Australian Feminist Studies** 10:49-69.

Strathern, Marilyn
  In press **After Nature: English Kinship in the Late Twentieth Century**. [Lewis Henry Morgan Lectures, University of Rochester]. Cambridge: Cambridge University Press.

Thornton, Robert
  1988a The Rhetoric of Ethnographic Holism. **Cultural Anthropology** 3:285-303.

Thorton, Robert
  1988b Time Scales and Social Thought. **Time and Mind: The Study of Time** IV, University of Mass. Press.

Tuzin, Donald F.
  1980 **The Voice of the Tamberan: Truth and Illusion in Ilahita Arapesh Religion**. Berkeley and Los Angeles: University of California Press.

Tuzin, Donald
  In press The Cryptic Brotherhood of Big Men and Great Men in Ilahita. In **Big Men and Great Men: The Development of a Comparison in Melanesia**, M. Godelier and M. Strathern (eds.). Cambridge: Cambridge University Press.

Tyler, Stephen A.
  1986 Post-Modern Ethnography: From Document of the Occult to Occult Document. In **Writing Culture: The Poetics and Politics of Ethnography**, J. Clifford and G. Marcus (eds.). Berkeley and Los Angeles: University of California Press.

Tyler, Stephen A. and Marcus, George E.
  1987 Comment on M. Strathern, The Persuasive Fictions of Anthropology. **Current Anthropology** 28:275-277.

Ulmer, George
  1985 The Object of Post-Criticism. In **Postmodern Culture**, H. Foster (ed.). London: Pluto Press.

Wagner, Roy
  1977 Scientific and Indigenous Papuan Conceptualizations of the Innate: A
  Semiotic Critique of the Ecological Perspective. In **Subsistence and
  Survival**, T. Bayliss-Smith and R. Feachem (eds.). London: Academic
  Press.

Wagner, Roy
  1986a **Symbols That Stand for Themselves**. Chicago: University of
  Chicago Press.

Wagner, Roy
  1986b **Asiwinarong: Ethos, Image, and Social Power among the Usen Barok
  of New Ireland**. Princeton: Princeton University Press.

Wagner, Roy
  1987 Figure-Ground Reversal among the Barok. In **Assemblage of Spirits:
  Idea and Image in New Ireland**, L. Lincoln (ed.). New York: Geo Braziller
  with The Minneapolis Institute of Arts.

Wagner, Roy
  In press The Fractal Person. In **Big Men and Great Men: The Development
  of a Comparison in Melanesia**, M. Godelier and M. Strathern (eds.).
  Cambridge: Cambridge University Press.

Wagner, Roy
  n.d. Culture and Order: A View from New Ireland. [Munro Lecture,
  University of Edinburgh, 1986.]

Webster, Steven
  1987 Structuralist Historicism and the History of Structuralism: Sahlins, the
  Hansons' 'Counterpoint in Maori Culture,' and Postmodernist
  Ethnographic Form. **Journal of Polynesian Society**. 96:27-65.

Weiner, Annette
  1982 Sexuality among the Anthropologists: Reproduction among the
  Informants. In **Sexual Antagonism, Gender, and Social Change in Papua
  New Guinea**, F.J.P. Poole and G. Herdt (eds.). **Social Analysis**
  (spec. issue) 12.

Weiner, James F.
  1987 Diseases of the Soul: Sickness, Agency and the Men's Cult among the
  Foi of New Guinea. In **Dealing with Inequality. Analysing Gender
  Relations in Melanesia and Beyond**, M. Strathern (ed.). Cambridge:
  Cambridge University Press.

Weiner, James F.
  1988 **The Heart of the Pearlshell: The Mythological Dimension of Foi Sociality**. Los Angeles and Berkeley: University of California Press.

Weiner, James F. (ed.)
  1988 **Mountain Papuans: Historical and Comparative Perspectives from New Guinea Fringe Highlands Societies**. Ann Arbor: University of Michigan Press.

Werbner, Richard P.
  1989 **Ritual Passage, Sacred Journey. The Process and Organization of Religious Movement**. Washington: Smithsonian Institute Press.

Werbner, Richard P.
  In press Trickster and the Eternal Return: Self-Reference in West Sepik World Renewal. In **Shooting the Sun**, B. Juillerat (ed.). Washington: Smithsonian Institution Press.

Wilden, Anthony
  1972 **System and Structure. Essays in Communication and Exchange**. London: Tavistock Publications.

Young, Michael
  1987 The Tusk, The Flute and the Serpent: Disguise and Revelation in Goodenough Mythology. In **Dealing with Inequality. Analysing Gender Relations in Melanesia and Beyond**, M. Strathern (ed.). Cambridge: Cambridge University Press.

18971589R00107

Printed in Great Britain
by Amazon